EXHIBIT *Like An* EXPERT

Sell More,
Look Great
&
Make Money

At Tradeshows,
Consumer Shows
and Events

By Susan Ratliff

Exhibit like an Expert
Sell More, Look Great & Make Money
At Tradeshows, Consumer Shows and Events

By Susan Ratliff

ISBN: 978-0-9796806-0-1

To receive additional copies of this book or to contact Susan Ratliff for consulting or speaking opportunities for your company or organization call 602-437-3634 or email her at susan@exhibitexpertsaz.com, or

For information about Exhibit Experts, tradeshow exhibits and displays go to www.exhibitexpertsaz.com

Acknowledgements

Many thanks to:

Larry Campbell, wherever you are, for taking me under your wing and teaching me all you knew about this exciting industry.

The talented staff at Exhibit Experts that makes this business grow and every customer who has used our services.

Graeme Nelson and the staff of American Displays and every product vendor and service provider who contributes to the success of my business.

Brandi Hollister for the outstanding cover design and Vickie Mullins at Mullins Creative for the book layout and valuable advice.

The associations, organizations and Chambers of Commerce that have assisted me with business challenges, sponsored my causes and supported me in my efforts to build a successful company. Thank you for continuing to provide ideal forums of information and education to small businesses everywhere.

To my husband, Carey, for his encouragement and patience throughout this project.

Table of contents

Acknowledgements i

Dear Exhibitor iv

Selecting Profitable Exhibiting Events I

Find the best shows • Tradeshow resources • Plan your
budget before the show • Determine your booth size and
type • Select your space • Classify the audience • Do your
homework • Stay on schedule

The Exhibitor Kit of Show Services 18

Booth space contract • Installation and dismantle
• Union labor • Save money • Drayage • Electrical service
• Photographer • Rental options • Fire regulations
• Cost-saving shipping secrets

Setting Goals for Best Results 30

Sell something • Get leads • Lead management • Investigate
the competition • Gather market research • Network
with exhibitors • Build your company image • Recruit
personnel • Feature something new • Prepare to get publicity
• Connect with your existing customer • Put it into action
• Show goal sheet

Create a Dynamic Display 45

Design around a theme • Integrate interesting props • Bigger
is better • It's a small world • Expand your space • Magnetic
merchandising • Dress up the staff • Grab them with graphics
• Keep text to a minimum • Go for the WOW factor • Think
off-the-wall • Use key colors • Create compelling graphics
• Producing graphics • Cost-saving tips for graphics • Prevent
graphic nightmares • Table covers • Turn on the lights •
Technology and tricks • Give your display the critical eye •
A word about booth security

Pick Your Perfect Structure or Style.................................67
Portable displays • Panel systems • Pop-up displays • Fabric exhibits • Banner stands • Accessories • Custom displays • Buying a display off the internet • Make it yourself • Shelves • Panels • Pegboards • Wire grids • Lattice • Modular wire cubes • Slat wall panels • Get organized • Get the most from your investment • Top ten tips for a terrific display

Drive Traffic to Your Booth................................79
Promotions before the show • Make it personal • Send it and they will come • Promotions at the show • Hold a demonstration • Give a live presentation • Put your customers to work • Feature a personality • Play a game-offer samples • Hold a drawing • Furnish give-aways • Teach a seminar • Use bag stuffers • Donate a door prize • Be a sponsor • Use door hangers • Hospitality suites • Program ads • Collateral and business cards

Sales Strategies for the Tradeshow Environment 94
Select your booth staff • Prepare your sales team • Your formula for selling success • The 5 E's for exhibitor selling – Engage, Excite, Educate, Encourage and Exit • Special tips for selling at consumer shows • Sales worksheet • Target your audience • Selling strategies • Independent selling • Team selling • Top trade show selling tips • Proper etiquette keeps you professional

Create an Effective Follow-up System 116
Say thank you • Make an announcement • Give preferred treatment • Take a survey • Ask for referrals • Share publicity • Solicit testimonials • Include a call to action • Calculate your ROI (Return on Investment)

The Exhibit Expert's Top Ten Tips 122

About the Author.. 123

Dear Exhibitor ~

Wouldn't you like to cut through the clutter of frustrating formulas, theoretical calculations and boring analysis about how to have a successful show? And get instead to the practical, cost-effective, easy to implement, tips and strategies that will give you immediate results everywhere you exhibit? Read this book today and your staff will sell better and get more qualified leads at every show. Follow these simple instructions and your display will look fabulous and make a lasting impression on attendees. Stick with these guidelines and your business will make a huge leap in returns on your investment at your very next exhibit marketing event.

In recent years, trends in marketing have changed drastically. We are bombarded daily with hundreds of advertisements from newspapers, magazines, radio and TV, but their effectiveness has diminished, because it is easy for anyone to tune out commercials with the channel changer, block phone solicitors, delete e-mail, or toss junk mail. Businesses are finding it much more difficult to reach and penetrate their target audiences.

What continues to work very well is face-to-face marketing, which can be described as the unique opportunity to meet a group of targeted prospects in one place at the same time. This is why many companies are increasing their use of temporary events to promote and sell their products and services. Business owners can find lucrative exhibit marketing choices close to home, around the country or around the world. Of the event marketing opportunities available, the superior benefits of consumer shows and tradeshows are substantiated by staggering statistics. The Center for Exhibition Industry Research has spent the last 25 years compiling this valuable information. When comparing tradeshows to field sales, direct mail, telemarketing, public relations or the internet, decision-makers select exhibitions as the #1 source of final purchases. This is because tradeshows are a convenient and fast way to find, evaluate and compare products and services. When the marketing objectives include generating leads, taking orders, promoting brand visibility, penetrating new markets or introducing new services, tradeshows and consumer shows are the most effective means to accomplish those goals. See more information and statistics about the exhibition industry at www.ceir.org.

Imagine yourself setting up for your next trade show. You eagerly erect your display, creatively position your graphics, attractively set out your literature and painstakingly position your products. Then, you think about spending ten hours a day standing on your feet until the show is over, at which point you must tear down your booth, and pack up everything for transport. At some point you've probably asked yourself why you bother to go through the exhaustive effort required to exhibit at trade shows. Do you consider exhibiting a necessary evil? Would you give up exhibiting all together if your competition wasn't in the aisle around the corner? Do you have a negative attitude about shows because you've never gotten the results you wanted or realized a measurable return on your investment? Do you believe that your money would be better spent on additional advertising, expanding the sales staff or improving phone prospecting instead of trade shows? Maybe you've never even considered exhibiting in an event before.

There are more than 11,000 tradeshows a year attended by 120 million people who spend more than 100 billion dollars. Nine out of ten companies ranked exhibitions as the #1 most useful source of purchasing information, because they could examine and evaluate competing products in one location. The four major industries that make up the tradeshow figures are manufacturing, healthcare, technology and food and beverage, but every type of business from any industry will have event marketing opportunities available. The Center for Exhibition Industry Research says you will reach seven times as many prospects at a tradeshow than you would through any other type of marketing, except field sales, and these leads cost you 61 percent less to close. In addition, the caliber of prospects attending a tradeshow is excellent. The Tradeshow Trends report compiled by Exhibit Surveys Research shows that this is an audience ready to spend money with your company. The following statistics about the average behaviors of attendees should convince you of the enormous value event marketing holds for your business.

- 52% come to buy something.

- 84% have buying influence.

- 29% are the decision makers.

- 26% will sign a purchase order.

- 94% will compare competing products.

- 78% have not been contacted by your company in the last twelve months.

Those statistics don't even include over 2,200 consumer shows taking place across the U.S. The consumer or public show, unlike the tradeshow, is always a forum that brings together retail sellers with the buying public. The most popular categories for consumer shows are sports, travel, entertainment, home repair, garden and professional business services. On average, 25,000 people will pass through the doors of a weekend consumer show. The average age of an attendee is between 30 and 59 with an annual income over $50,000. Public shows attract both loyal customers and new prospects willing to buy now and in the future.

Here is what researchers have discovered about this specific group of attendees:

- 95% are decision makers.

- 73% have attended the show an average of six other times.

- 27% will be first time attendees.

- 37% will purchase products at the show.

- 59% will purchase within a year.

Expand your marketing reach with tradeshows. It's not hard to notice that small businesses are greatly affected by turbulent economic times. Turn on the TV or open a newspaper and you are confronted with reports of cutbacks, layoffs and bankruptcies. When capital is in short supply, the tendency for most small companies is to slash the marketing and advertising budgets. It is with this knowledge that the shrewd corporation or business owner seizes the opportunity to increase market share and get an edge on the competition. While everyone else is waiting it out, the smart entrepreneur is finding new ways to reach their customers. One of the most effective ways to capitalize on a down market is through a tradeshow. Big business has been capitalizing on the benefits of exhibit marketing for years. With a little knowledge and some careful planning, even the smallest business can tap into this lucrative marketplace.

I didn't know a thing about exhibit marketing back in October 1988 when I started a home-based children's book business after the birth of my son. For six years I carted a computer and book making supplies from backyard craft fairs to convention center trade shows and outdoor swap meets. I sold my products at every temporary vending event I could find. By promoting and selling my products at many types of exhibiting venues, I learned first hand what skills were required to be an exhibit expert and made hundreds of mistakes along the way. This book was written to save you from making all the mistakes I made and to provide you with the knowledge, skills and techniques that will help you capitalize on the value of exhibit marketing. Whether you're a professional speaker, a recruiter, a representative of a large corporation, an entrepreneur, home-based business owner or a non-profit entity, event marketing offers everyone equal access to and personal contact with a large number of focused buyers in one captive setting. In this easy-to-follow workbook, you will learn how to locate and select the most profitable shows for your business and how to design a dynamic display that will attract your target audience. You will receive tips on booking booth space and planning your event schedule. Also included are successful sales strategies to increase profits, tools for developing clever promotions, techniques to increase lead generation, effective follow-up methods, the means with which to calculate a return on your investment and much more.

Don't wait another minute to capitalize on the billion dollar event industry. Remember what Zig Zigler says, "If you always do what you've always done, you'll always get what you've always gotten." Follow the instructions offered and implement the techniques provided, and you will increase your effectiveness and maximize your profits at every trade show, convention, job fair, consumer show and temporary vending event you participate in.

SR

Selecting Profitable Exhibiting Events

T he exhibit industry is enormous. With more than 13,500 trade shows, consumer shows, job fairs, craft shows and conventions to chose from in the U.S. and around the world, it is essential to select shows that will generate the most profit and sales for your products and services. Take time to plan your exhibit strategy. Pay careful attention to the details outlined in this chapter. They will keep you from making costly mistakes and will put you on the road to success and profits quickly. All shows are not created equal, so before you pay an entry fee to exhibit, take time to study the elements that make a show successful. By understanding what makes one show better than another, you will be able to pick shows that will minimize risk and maximize profits for your business. Remember, the best shows are those in which the exhibitor can qualify the audience, accomplish specific goals and obtain a quantifiable return on the investment.

Finding the best shows

There are a variety of publications and websites available that will assist you in compiling a list of events. Unfortunately, there is no single source or comprehensive list of all the exhibiting opportunities for businesses that will draw the correct targeted audience that will accomplish your business goals. There are several publications that provide a variety of helpful information, such as show name, organizer, contact person, show dates, locations and types of attendees and exhibitors. Some provide show history, projected attendance, attendee profiles and show analysis. Events are indexed either chronologically, alphabetically, geographically or by industry or profession.

Finding exhibit marketing opportunities in your local area involves some research. Look first to your local daily newspapers. Many event promoters will advertise shows there. Contact the convention centers and large hotels in your area to inquire about what events they host.

Your Chambers of Commerce and Convention and Visitors Bureaus will most likely offer a list of shows. Many such organizations produce their own business expos. Read the trade journals of your target industries. Be sure to call your suppliers to get their recommendations of what shows they attend and don't hesitate to find out where your competition is exhibiting.

Whether you attend a show as an attendee or an exhibitor, make a point to talk to other exhibitors that target your same buying audience and inquire which shows have been successful for them. Experienced exhibitors are a great source of useful information and are often willing to share their knowledge. Consumer shows will always be advertised in the media. Read and listen for opportunities and contact the promoters of the show to request an exhibitor packet.

Many events take place annually and are produced by the same organizations each time. Compile your own private list of events that have been successful for you. Chances are the contacts and information will remain the same year after year. When you find a show you like, that provides the return you are after, consider booking your space for the following year, before the show is over. Many promoters encourage early sign-ups and provide discounts and incentives in exchange for your prompt commitment. If they don't offer an incentive, ask for one. If you have booked into a show consistently for many years you should consider yourself an important asset to the promoter. Request a discount off the price of your booth space or ask for a larger space if you book your booth early. Use early booking to leverage special privileges for preferred booth selection, special advertising rates or the opportunity to put something into the attendee bags. Offer to be an advocate for the show. Tell the promoter they can give your name out to potential exhibitors and you will provide a positive testimonial to encourage a prospect to purchase a booth in the show. Your loyalty and longevity as a happy exhibitor is valuable to the promoter. Use it to your advantage.

TRADESHOW RESOURCES

Exhibitor Magazine www.ExhibitorOnline.com

Expo Magazine www.expoweb.com

Tradeshow Central www.TSCentral.com

Tradeshow News Network www.TSNN.com

Pro Shows www.Proshows.com,

National Association of Consumer Shows
www.publicshows.com

International Shows www.eventseye.com

Healthcare www.HCEA.org

Technology www.techweb.com

Virtual Tradeshows www.goXpo.com

Plan your budget before the show

The next category that will drive your show selection decision
will be your budget. If your business or organization has
experience with exhibiting, then you are probably well past
the sticker shock that comes with finding out that there are
many more costs involved in participating in a show than just
buying a space, building a booth and sending the staff with it. If
you are not careful, your well-planned budget could explode
as a result of unforeseen expenses. If you are new to this
marketing avenue, this chapter might be a real eye-opener for
you and your team. If your show participation consists only of
shows you could drive to and set up yourself you will need to
carefully review this list of charges before booking booth
space at an out-of-state event. When you are armed with the
knowledge and details of what it will cost you to exhibit, then
you can prepare early and make a plan to cut those costs
using the tips in this chapter.

BUDGET CONSIDERATIONS

THE DISPLAY

Booth space _____
Exhibit design services _____
Exhibit hardware _____
Exhibit lighting _____
Exhibit shipping _____
Containers or crates _____
Exhibit refurbishing _____
Exhibit accessories _____
Exhibit rentals _____
Graphic design _____
Graphic production _____

FREIGHT AND TRANSPORTATION

Common Carrier (UPS/FEDEX) _____
Custom van lines _____
Lift gate _____
Wait time _____
Padding _____
Special delivery fees _____

SHOW SERVICES

Installation and Dismantle (I&D) _____
Supervisor for I&D _____
Electrical _____
Electrical labor _____
Internet _____
AV equip _____

Telephony _____
Cable TV _____
Plumbing _____
Compressed air _____
Gas _____
Water _____
Drayage dock to booth in and out _____
Warehousing _____
Cleaning _____
Floral _____
Furniture _____
Accessories _____
Photography _____
Security _____

STAFFING

Staff pay _____
Out of office expenses _____
Training _____
Employee incentives _____
Airfare/transportation _____
Lodging _____
Meals _____
Stipends _____
Premium give-aways _____
Hospitality suite _____
Client entertainment _____
Demonstration talent _____
Presenter's fees _____

Determine your booth size and type

There are conflicting opinions as to which spaces in an exhibit hall are the best. Below are some examples of the types and sizes of booth spaces and display areas available. The average single booth size is 10' deep x 10' wide x 8' high with 3' high side rails and 8' high back rails draped with curtains to designate each space. Exhibit size is expanded from the 10' x 10' size by adding spaces side by side, back to back or on opposite sides of the aisle from one another. Below are a variety of space sizes and descriptions.

Inline

The standard inline booth is one that is back to back with another where one side faces the traffic aisle while the other two sides and the back connect to neighbors. This space consists of 8' x 10' or 10' x 10' size areas that may not exceed 8' in height along the back wall or more than 5' toward the aisle. The remaining 5' to the aisle is limited to 3' in height. These spaces are the least expensive, but one disadvantage is that attendees cannot see your entire exhibit until they are right in front of your booth. There is a tendency by exhibitors in this size space to place a table across the front that creates a barrier between you and the customer. It is not uncommon to see two people sitting behind a table covered with literature or merchandise. It would be much more beneficial if the staff could greet prospects and invite them into the booth from a smaller, more friendly counter.

Cross aisle

Two standard linear spaces on opposite sides of the aisle from one another allows your company to capture the entire flow of attendees traveling through the aisle in front of each space.

Corner

If you can only afford an inline space make a point to book early so you can obtain a corner spot. This is an inline booth with one side open in addition to the front. Corner spots are very desirable and often come with a premium 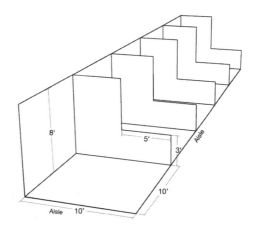 attached, but it is worth it to pay extra for a corner booth when possible. Be sure that you remove the side rail on the corner aisle for maximum exposure and to encourage attendees to enter from that side.

Peninsula

The peninsula has aisle space open on three sides with the rear wall connecting to a neighbor. A maximum display height of 8' along the back wall is permitted. However, the 8' height is limited to the center 10' of the back 20' of wall space and must drop to 3' 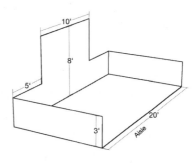 in height only on the remaining 5' of each side of the aisle to ensure that the view of your neighbors to the rear is not blocked. There are some shows that will allow the entire rear 20' wall to be used. Read your exhibitor kit from show services to confirm all booth space details.

Island

An island space is open to customer traffic on all four sides. The minimum size of an island exhibit is 20' x 20'. Aisles separate the island from other booths and the exhibiting 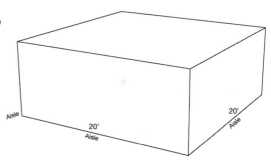 company controls the air space above the booth. This means that by selecting an island booth, you get permission to extend your exhibit up higher than an inline booth permits. You can also hang signs or graphics from the ceiling over your booth space or extend your display or signs as high as 16-20', so they can be seen from any area of the exhibit hall.

Select your space

If you want to make sure you get the best possible booth location for your business you will need to purchase your space as early as possible. When reviewing the floor plan for a prime spot think about how the traffic will flow into the hall. Most attendees walk to the right when entering the exhibit area. Calculate how they will travel around the floor so you will know from what direction they will approach your booth. Find out where your competitors will be setting up. It would be best to locate yourself out of direct site of any competing company. Where will attendees congregate for special events, demonstrations or entertainment? Be aware that certain activities will draw large crowds that may block your exhibit from the view of attendees for long periods of time. Such activities might be noisy and distracting as well. Where are the food concessions, lounge areas and rest rooms located? Some people think selecting a booth that aligns with the path a person will travel to reach those destinations is a benefit.

Others think that locating your company across from these areas will have attendees staring at your company and products for extended periods of time. How does traffic flow from the workshops or seminars? You could receive additional bursts of interest if there are hundreds of people passing your booth multiple times during the show. It is safe to assume that everyone who attends the tradeshow or consumer show will pass by your booth at least once, no matter where you are. It is then up to you to capture them at your exhibit.

Areas to avoid

The following is a list of locations in the exhibit hall that may pose problems for your staff or present difficulties when you erecting your display. If there are any indications of these on the floor plan, call show services to make sure there will not be a problem and to get a clear understanding of any restrictions.

- Dead-end aisles

- Low ceilings

- Walls and sight barriers

- Poorly lit areas

- Columns, posts and pilings

- Loading docks and freight doors

- Late set-up areas

- Split aisles

- Power, water and air sources

Classify the audience

Before you select your next event, you must classify the type of exhibitors and attendees that will be present to determine whether a show will meet your needs. There are two show classifications, horizontal and vertical. Understanding their differences will help you estimate how many customers will be interested in your product and, therefore, better help you to market your products and services. In a vertical show the exhibitors target a single market or industry. For example, exhibitors at the National Physical Therapists Association show are selling products used exclusively by physical therapists in hospitals and private practice. It is a vertical show for the healthcare industry marketing to physical therapists. The audience is also vertical coming from a single industry, in this case, physical therapists themselves or hospital representatives. Horizontal shows are those where the mix of exhibitors sell a diverse array of products and services that appeal to a wide variety of attendees. A Home and Garden show, for example, features exhibitors selling everything from swimming pools, lighting fixtures, appliances, plants and furniture to those selling insurance, banking services and cellular phones. The attendees will come with a variety of needs as varied as the offerings; therefore they are horizontal as well.

How does this information affect your show selection? When you determine whether the exhibitors and attendees are either horizontal or vertical you will be better able to evaluate the Audience Interest Factor (AIF). According to Richard Swanby, founder of Exhibit Survey's Inc., the AIF is a way to measure visitor interest and the ability of exhibits to attract visitors. His observations have shown that the AIF is higher for vertical seller shows than for horizontal seller shows because a show attendee is more apt to visit exhibits pertaining to his special interests than unrelated exhibits. His findings conclude that Vertical Seller-Vertical Buyer shows have the highest AIF, while Horizontal Seller-Vertical Buyer shows have the lowest AIF.

Do your homework

There is no bigger waste of time and money than buying a booth in a show that's not right for your business. Unfortunately, many companies select shows in such random fashion that they end up in the wrong event quite often. Some businesses don't bother analyzing results of participation and continue to spend wasted dollars staying in shows that should be removed from their list. Here are a few suggestions to help you avoid making mistakes with your show selection.

- Make a list of shows you would like to exhibit in. Before you spend money participating in unfamiliar events, visit as many shows as possible as a customer to first analyze whether it will be a good fit for your company, products and services.

- Consider the location of the venue. Is it convenient to the audience? Is it easily accessible to your target audience? Is parking free and plentiful or will attendees be required to pay? Is the event site visible from the street and does it include directional signage?

- Take notes to find out if the show has the dynamics that meet the needs of your company. Is there enough foot traffic? Study the characteristics of the crowd to see if they fit your customer profile. Do the attendees seem pleased? Are they making purchases or simply looking?

- Examine the merchandise and services displayed. Would your products and services complement the show and fit in well with the other offerings? Does the quality of goods being showcased compare in quality and variety to what you have to offer?

• Check the promoter's track record. A promoter's show experience can have a great impact on the success of an event. A show that repeats year after year will have a strong customer following and a good mix of vendors. Shows held for three years or more are likely to run smoothly. Find out about past attendance and compare it to the information stated in the marketing materials. First time shows require scrutiny.

• Is the promoter meeting the needs of the exhibitors? The show is only as good as the management behind it. Make sure the event management's goal is to make you successful. How are qualified attendees and buyers being driven to the tradeshow? Is there a major corporate sponsor participating? Is there a Charity angle? Are there opportunities for exhibitors to receive publicity in newspapers or on the radio through new product showcases or press releases? Is there an aggressive advertising campaign using multiple forms of media for attracting your target audience? Are there options for additional exposure to attendees such as program ads, sponsorships, bag stuffers, door hangers or speaking opportunities? Does the organizer provide exhibitors with marketing tools like flyers or inserts they can distribute, stickers to put on mailings or admission tickets to pass out to prospects and customers?

• Observe the exhibitors participating in the event. Ask them if they are pleased with the show and if they would exhibit there again. What is their attitude towards the promoter, location, people attending, quality of prospects and the number of sales they've made? Ask them how many years they have participated in the show. If they are disgruntled, but continue to exhibit year after year, then the show probably holds value to them. Ask the promoter to provide you with the names and phone numbers of past exhibitors you can contact for references.

- Count the number of direct competitors participating. Find out if the show has been beneficial to them and how many years they've participated. Make sure you can get a booth far enough away from them.

- Look over the floor plan. Make note of any undesirable booth spaces. Select a few spots that would be ideal for your company when you decide to book the show. Look over the venue, parking situation and convenience to hotels, shopping and amenities.

If you are not inclined to visit the show in person prior to committing to buying a booth, then research the answers on the event website. Savvy promoters will provide a list of exhibitors with links to their websites so you can check out products and services being offered, quality of goods and number of competitors. Look for information on past history pertaining to the show's success, such as reprints of articles or publicity the show received. Call the management office and get all your questions answered before you move forward.

With your personal research, information obtained from the promoters and the demographic information provided by the show directories and websites provided here, you should have the knowledge necessary to successfully select the shows that will attract the most qualified buyers for your product or service.

Stay on schedule

The smart exhibitor knows the advantage of preparing for each event in advance. Careful attention to details here will pay off big in the long run. Planning ahead can save you a substantial amount of money over the course of a season. Ordering exhibit services and supplies early will allow you to take advantage of prepayment discounts and prevent last-minute overcharges. Waiting until the last minute to order a new display, produce graphics or purchase your promotional gifts could result in unnecessary rush charges and high shipping costs. If you don't prepare early you will leave little time to work with the display and catch any mistakes that may have occurred. Use this simple planning guide so you will have peace of mind that your exhibit will end up as impressive as it should be and the show will run smoothly. I suggest you design a chart that has columns listing the activity, the deadline to complete it and the person assigned to accomplish it. This will provide a timeline and spell out the specific duties that must be distributed to all parties involved.

TWELVE MONTHS IN ADVANCE

☐ Review the list of shows that your company should exhibit in.

☐ Check to see if booth space is available for the shows you desire.

☐ Visit those shows as an attendee to personally evaluate them.

SIX MONTHS IN ADVANCE

☐ Establish your budget for each show.

☐ Confirm every exhibiting event in which you will participate.

☐ Reserve the booth space in the shows you select.

EXHIBIT I

FOUR MONTHS IN ADVANCE

❏ Establish goals for the show and assign t. team member.

❏ Decide on the marketing theme and begin designing display graphics.

❏ Set up your existing display to review its condition.

❏ If you will purchase a new display begin visiting potential vendors.

❏ Plan for the collateral you will take to the show.

❏ Review the exhibitor packet from the show promoter.

❏ Make a checklist of what items must be ordered, then order early.

❏ Begin selecting exhibit staff.

❏ Hold a meeting with both the sales and marketing departments to brainstorm your plan of action and marketing message.

THREE MONTHS IN ADVANCE

❏ Finalize the work schedule for the exhibit staff.

❏ Make hotel and travel arrangements.

❏ Finalize the theme and marketing messages for graphics.

❏ Select and order give-aways that tie into the marketing plan.

❏ Determine if a pre-show promotion will be used to advertise and coordinate it with the booth theme.

❏ Place advertising and begin ordering supplies for pre-show mailers.

- ☐ Review layout for booth configuration.
- ☐ Write press releases and create a list of media contacts.

TWO MONTHS IN ADVANCE

- ☐ Complete the work schedule and distribute duties and goals to staff.
- ☐ Brainstorm with the sales staff to develop a sales strategy and list potential objections that clients may mention at the show.
- ☐ Script the presentation along with objection rebuttals and distribute to the booth staff for memorization.
- ☐ Review the budget.
- ☐ Order booth graphics, display items and print materials.
- ☐ Finalize all services needed for the show and order them.
- ☐ Provide shipping information to vendors.
- ☐ Schedule installation and dismantle services if necessary.
- ☐ Finalize travel and hotel arrangements for the staff.

ONE MONTH IN ADVANCE

- ☐ Create a VIP guest list, write and mail invitations.
- ☐ Hold a staff training session to review sales strategy and presentations.
- ☐ Confirm all ordered items are on schedule for delivery.
- ☐ Set up the exhibit and have the staff review for functionality.

☐ Make final decisions on display shipping schedule.

TWO WEEKS IN ADVANCE

☐ Make checklist of items to be taken to show.

☐ Organize and pack supplies, tickets, service orders etc. to be sent in advance.

☐ Check on the progress of the display and graphics.

☐ Obtain checks or credit cards to be used for on-site expenses and payments.

AT THE SHOW BEFORE OPENING

☐ Arrive early to register and pick up show ID badges.

☐ Confirm arrival of exhibit, equipment and services.

☐ Meet with I & D supervisor regarding booth set-up.

☐ Conduct pre-show briefing with staff and review goals.

DURING THE SHOW

☐ Conduct daily meetings to assess progress and organize leads.

☐ Reserve next year's booth space.

☐ Make arrangements to dismantle and ship your exhibit.

☐ Supervise the break down of the display and confirm shipping at end of show.

AFTER THE SHOW

☐ Distribute show leads to the staff for follow up.

☐ Write thank-you notes.

☐ Hold post-show sales debriefing and brainstorm areas to improve.

☐ Confirm procedure for calculating return on investment.

The Exhibitor Kit of
Show Services

When you make a commitment to exhibit in an expo, you will receive an exhibitor's kit from the promoter or the show decorator that is managing the event. It may be mailed as a hard copy, but most likely will be accessible on line. When the exhibitor kit is available on a website you have the opportunity to read the entire kit, but only print those forms you need.

The kit will consist of page after page of instructions, restrictions and rules you must follow as an exhibitor. It will also include helpful information, critical deadlines and important order forms that, if read and followed in a timely manner, will save you time, money and headaches. I suggest you create an on site book for every show. This can be a folder or a binder that will have copies of all the pertinent documents, signed forms, authorizations, certificates, contact persons, billing information and payment permissions for everything you need. Document all communications with everyone pertaining to the show and keep all their contact information in this file for easy reference. Following are some of the most important areas of information covered in the kit.

Booth space contract

Be sure to read this document carefully to ensure that you understand exactly what is included with your booth fee. It should state the date, the location where the event will be held, the hours of the show, what types of businesses are eligible to exhibit, restrictions, payment deadlines and cancellation policies. The agreement will include a floor plan of the show, your booth number, space size and location and the items included in the booth fee such as an 8' draped table, carpet, sign, chairs, wastebasket and electrical outlets. There may be height, dimension, lighting and sound restrictions or limitations, too. Also take note of any promotional restrictions on the types of give-aways, contests, drawings, costumes, noise level and literature you can distribute. Sometimes these require special approval from show management and you may not be permitted to promote outside your space.

Installation and dismantle

In the kit there will be specific times assigned to your company for setting up and taking down your display. This is particularly important due to the enormous number of companies that must bring in exhibits through the loading docks. If the show is local and you have a portable exhibit you will be setting up by yourself, you might be permitted to drive your vehicle onto the dock and unload your merchandise, but you must then remove and park your vehicle before you can return to take your things to your booth. If you are shipping exhibit materials, you will need to make arrangements for services such as warehousing, delivery, drayage and labor. Each is explained in detail in this chapter.

Union labor

In many states, labor unions rule the trade show convention

halls and you cannot so much as plug in a light fixture without paying a union worker. You are permitted to set up your booth by yourself, provided one person can do so in thirty minutes or less with no tools. This time restriction is unrealistic for most exhibitors. Otherwise, you must consent to use union workers and the documentation outlining rates and rules will be provided in the Exhibitor Kit. Union rates are usually very expensive averaging $75 per hour, per worker during regular business hours, increasing to overtime after 4:00 PM and time and a half on weekends and holidays. Along with the labor rates comes the cost of equipment rentals. If you need to place a header on your center kiosk you might need a forklift. To hang shelves you might need to rent a ladder. Hanging signs above an exhibit will require a scissor lift. The use of any of the show services equipment necessary to complete your installation and dismantle will result in a charge to you.

If you cannot or do not wish to set up your exhibit yourself, and don't want to pay union labor there is a very important page in your exhibitor kit you will want to pull out as soon as possible. It is the Non-Official Contractor form. This form allows you to hire an outside company of your choice. These non-official contractors must present certain business information and provide a certificate of insurance to the convention services company or decorator, in charge of the show. When you arrange for labor you are taking money out of the pockets of the convention services company so rules and deadlines must be strictly followed. The non-official contractor paperwork must be in the hands of the decorator thirty days before the show so make it a point to send it well in advance of the deadline to prevent any problems. Keep copies and records of all paperwork and communications. Call to confirm your documents were received by show management, because if they do not have a copy on file by the due date, then your contract labor or staff will not be permitted to build your display and you will be forced to pay the labor rates of the contractor.

Save money

Pack several sets of setup instructions inside your exhibit cases. Include pictures of the completed booth in all configurations you normally use. Take pictures from several different angles for clarity. Show details of where counters, shelves, monitors and computers are located. Include pictures of all graphic applications and where graphics should be mounted. Send along a touch up kit with paint, cleaning supplies, rags, assembly tools and a hand vacuum. Get the cell phone number of any contract laborers or supervisor and give them yours. Make sure a dependable staff member sets a time to meet the exhibit installers to confirm the proper booth configuration and graphic positioning. Hiring your own installation supervisor would be wise. If the laborers set up your exhibit incorrectly or different from your preference because there were no instructions in the crates or they were difficult to decipher it could be very costly to take it down and reinstall everything.

Drayage

If you wish to ship your crates and containers of show materials in advance, you will need to contract drayage services. Drayage is the service of moving your freight from the loading dock to your booth space then picking up your empty shippers, storing them and returning them to your booth when the show is over. In a small event at a hotel you may be permitted to store a few cases behind your booth or under a table, but this will not be the case at most convention halls.

Drayage is an expensive service, billed according to the weight of your shipments. The fees average $1 per pound of weight with a minimum of 100lbs. The key to saving money on this service is keeping accurate documentation on the weight of your freight. If such documentation is not available, the company can weigh your containers themselves and charge fees from those numbers. Obtain a weight ticket from your freight carrier and always check it against the drayage bills to prevent overcharges. Ship everything in advance in one shipment to minimize weight charges. Document everything and keep copies of all forms in a show folder and bring it with you to the show.

Electrical service

There will be a special order form in your kit pertaining to electrical services. There is usually a separate company working with the show decorator to provide all the electrical needs. You must calculate and determine your voltage, wattage and amp requirements before you fill out the order. It's easy to count your watts from your bulbs in the lighting fixtures you use, but if you plan to bring video equipment, computers, or multi-media electronics, it's best to consult your audiovisual provider or speak to the electrical contractor first. Consider the amount of electrical cords that you will need to run everything. If there are too many thick cords that will cause a hazard if run under the carpet, you might be required to pay for a ceiling drop where the electric connection comes from above into your display. There are new flat electrical extension cords now available too. Take advantage of special discounts by ordering early. Bring your own extension cords, converters, bulbs and attachments so you will not have to rent anything at the last minute. The electric company is only responsible for bringing service to your booth. You will again be charged for labor to lay the lines. Do not plug in any electrical cords or run any wires without first checking with the electric supplier.

Photographer

An attractive photo of your exhibit can be a useful marketing tool. In addition, it is a great help for employees and the set-up crew to see how the display looks when assembled. You can hire the show photographer to take an assortment of different views in color or black and white. Prices average about $50 per view. The photographer's lens angles and lighting produce much better quality photographs than those taken by you at the show.

Rental options

In addition to those things already mentioned, your kit will include a variety of order forms for rental items such as nightly cleaning services, security guards, floral items, furniture, carpeting, telephones, food service, plumbing services, electronic lead retrieval machines, hostesses and audio-video equipment. Send your order in early to capture discounts of some services. Any items rented from show services are going to be very expensive and extremely costly if you forget to order in advance and must rent them the day of the show. You can save a small fortune by bringing your own portable hand vacuum, cleaning supplies, silk plants, carpeting, table covers and light bulbs.

Fire regulations

Most shows require exhibitors to comply with strict fire safety rules and regulations established by local authorities. Make sure all display materials in your booth are fire retardant. The district Fire Marshal often does on-site, random flame tests at many shows. This means the Marshal may come to your booth and ask to see written proof that your display, table coverings, accessories and decorations are constructed of fire retardant materials. If you cannot provide such proof he will place a lighted match to the bottom of your table covering or display fabric to see if it will burn. If you have purchased your display and accessories from a professional display company you can assume everything is flame retardant. Most companies provide you with the documentation when you make the purchase. If you've built your own display, you can apply a variety of spray-on or wash-in flame retardant products to your exhibit materials or hire a company to do it for you. Look in the Yellow Pages under "flame proofing" for companies specializing in this service and at the hardware stores for the self-application types. Many dry cleaners can flameproof any fabric accessories.

Cost-saving shipping secrets

The best way to save time and money is to plan ahead. Don't underestimate the amount of money it can cost you to ship your tradeshow display and supplies. The following information will help prevent sticker shock and teach you strategies that will ensure your freight arrives on time, free of damage with the least cost to you.

Portable tradeshow displays are designed to pack in cases that will ship UPS and FedEx or can be checked as luggage on an airplane. The airlines change their shipping rules frequently, so expect the possibility of being charged an additional fee to ship on your commercial flight. Putting your portable shippers on the plane and carting them around the airport and in the taxi might save you money, but it is an inconvenient experience. Consider shipping your materials by truck to reduce problems.

Custom exhibits will require trucking to and from the event. Working with a trucking company experienced with tradeshow shipments is critical to your bottom line. They often offer a dedicated trade shows division that provides solutions for companies that ship to and from temporary events. Trade show shipping is very different from the motor carrier shipping that is familiar to most carriers. Trade show shipments rarely take place on predictable schedules and each destination is different. Requirements of the decorator, labor schedules and delivery restrictions can cause unforeseen complications. An experienced tradeshow materials shipper can help you plan a shipping strategy that might save you time, money and wear and tear on your booth. A good transporter will provide little known shipping tips like loading your carpeting last so it comes out first to speed up your set up. They will provide a twenty-four hour hot-line phone number in case of emergencies. Their drivers will know the quickest routes and the locations of the marshalling yards used by the most popular exhibit halls. They can coordinate shipping to multiple shows and even store the display in between events to save money.

Please share the following recommendations and information with your tradeshow manager and everyone involved with shipping your display materials before you begin developing your transportation plan.

- **Read your Exhibit Kit thoroughly**. Review your kit as soon as it arrives and note discounts and dates available for early ordering of needed items. Note the move in and move out schedules to maximize cost savings when scheduling shipments. Be sure to send in the Independent Contractors permission form if you will not be hiring the decorator's labor force. Don't forget to calculate the cost of drayage (getting your crates from the dock to the booth). Make special note of the material handling forms. Take time to fill out your bill of lading and prepare shipping labels to and from the show. The bill of lading must be filed at the service desk before the end of the show. If you need help filling out forms or have any questions call your exhibit house or the person at the service desk at the show.

- **Insurance.** ALWAYS make sure you have adequate coverage. Check with your carrier to be sure your exhibit is covered during transit. Identify the box that carries all the value.

- **Provide your carrier with complete dimensions and weights.** This advance information will dictate the size and type of the truck, which could save you money. Your containers will be reweighed by the carrier and convention decorator. Request a truck with a lift gate, especially if you have containers on wheels, to save the cost of a forklift.

- **Schedule pickup and deliveries to and from the show site for the earliest possible weekday time.** This will save on wait time charges that occur when the driver sits on the dock waiting his turn and most importantly, your shipment won't be loaded or unloaded on overtime rates which average $75 to $125 per hour. Provide cell phone numbers of contact persons that the driver can reach if needed. Take the shipping company's 24 hour service number with you to the show.

- **Packaging your materials.** Crates and customized containers designed for trade show shipping are most likely to escape damage. Before you get packing, check your containers and make repairs or replacements. Never ship reused or worn boxes. Sturdy shipping containers are an investment that will pay for themselves. Over-sized items should never exceed the length of a pallet. Custom booths and some equipment and products may require pad wrap services. This requires very specialized handling and will increase your cost, not only with shipping and labor but also higher material handling rates. Consider purchasing roto-molded shipping containers or crates if at all possible, especially if you are shipping to numerous shows. If shipping numerous items, you may benefit from palletizing everything and covering it with shrink-wrap. Finally, take a photo of each container on the outside and on the inside to show how the fully packed display should look. Keep these photos with the set up instructions as a reference of how to repack the display.

- **Labeling your items.** Even if you palletize boxes and containers, be sure to put the shipping address on the outside of every container you will be shipping. For extra security consider putting labels inside your cases and crates too. Include all information on labels including the exhibit hall, number of crates, and all contact information. Don't only write the initials of the show name, but spell out the entire name of the show.

- **Send freight advanced to the warehouse.** Shipping your freight ahead of time to the convention services warehouse will save you a lot of headaches. Look for the special window of shipping dates and times in your exhibitor kit. Drivers don't have to wait and freight can be delivered Monday thru Friday during normal business hours. The material handling rates may be slightly higher, but savings will result because you will have no wait time charges as well as special charges that usually incur when shipping direct to show. In addition, your exhibit will be waiting for you in your booth so you can easily schedule staff and I &D people.

- **Ship direct to show site.** Always advise your shipping company if your show is targeted, which means that you have a specific time schedule to move your freight in and out. Make every effort to schedule deliveries during your target date and time to avoid additional expenses. If the show is not targeted, you should schedule your shipment to arrive at the earliest possible time. If your move-in time is between 8 am and 4 pm, schedule delivery for 8am. Shipments received late in the afternoon will probably be off-loaded on overtime rates by the decorator. Wait time usually increases the later the driver checks in to the marshalling yard, as drivers are usually taken on a first come, first serve basis. It's always best to have the driver check in as early as possible to minimize wait time whether you are moving in or out of a show.

- **Schedule outbound pickups the morning after the show breaks.** Instead of waiting around for your containers to be returned to your booth, which can take up to eight hours after the show closes, or scheduling the dismantle labor too early and rushing to pack up, consider having everything picked up first thing the next day.

- **Move-out.** Nothing happens until proper material handling forms are filled out and turned in. Always state your carrier of choice by writing your carrier's name on the Bill of Lading. Use the pre-printed waybill and labels provided by your carrier. Return completed paperwork to the service desk before you depart. Never leave your paperwork at the booth. If proper paperwork is not filled out on time or there are delays with your shipper your freight may be forced. This means the convention services company takes over your freight and ships it by their carrier. If this happens you can expect charges up to three times the cost of what you might have paid. You will pay your trucking company and the decorators.

Setting Goals for Best Results

Before you decide to purchase a display, design your marketing message or book booth space at an event, you must define your objectives and set goals that will achieve the results that you want. Most business owners and managers consider selling to be the primary purpose for exhibiting at a trade show. More often than not, the event is a showcase for products and services and affords buyers and sellers the opportunity to do business by purchase order for delivery after the event. Some shows prohibit the exchange of money and merchandise. They serve only as a lead gathering venue and a showcase for image building. Consumer shows offer direct retailing opportunities where products are sold and delivered to the customer at the booth. Even when sales are permitted, products that are expensive or not easily carried away from the show might be very difficult to sell at the show.

Your company's commitment to participate in a show should be followed by a commitment to get results. It is essential, before the show, that you know what you want to accomplish, have realistic expectations, make the staff aware of your goals and prepare them with the tools and knowledge to achieve them. In addition to closing a sale, there are many benefits your company can derive from participating in trade shows and consumer or public shows. Maximize your time and investment by first establishing a list of all the goals you wish to accomplish. Setting specific goals will help focus your efforts and give the booth staff a better understanding of what is expected of them. The more goals they have to accomplish the greater their chances for success. Goal setting assures that even if the sales fall short of expectations, you will gain valuable information about the competition, fresh marketing ideas, new suppliers, more qualified leads and the ability to calculate the return on your investment.

Most companies never establish any goals for the booth staff. There might be a short conversation about selling or getting leads, but rarely is there a pre-planned effort to craft a comprehensive set of objectives to guarantee more sales and profits for your company. Following is a list of eleven options to consider. Select the ones that best meet the needs of your business and implement them at your next show.

#1 – Sell something

If you are a business that sells products and services at consumer or public shows, then selling will be your most important goal. Your profits are directly tied to your ability to capture the customer's attention, engage them in conversation, qualify and close them on the spot. Participants in industry or business oriented tradeshows consider selling to be the primary purpose for exhibiting, but more often than not, the event is not a selling show, but simply a show case for products and services. This venue simply affords buyers and sellers the opportunity to evaluate goods and possibly write up a purchase order for delivery after the event. Some shows prohibit the exchange of money and merchandise altogether.

They serve only as a lead gathering opportunity. Even when sales are permitted, it is very difficult to actually close a sale on the show floor. This is especially true for expensive or complex products and services with long sales cycles. Strategies for developing sales presentations that work are outlined in detail in another chapter.

*#2 Get leads

Trade shows provide the opportunity to meet and speak with hundreds of potential customers. Some are qualified prospects that could become sales in the near future. Others will require some time to capitalize on their value and many will be uninterested in your offerings. Instead of making long sales presentations to a small number of potential customers, you should evaluate and qualify as many people as possible for detailed follow-up later on. There are many effective ways to acquire a name, address, phone number and email address. You can hold a drawing, have a contest or take a survey. You can also have attendees sign a guest book or be put on a list to receive your newsletter. Another option is to rent an electronic lead-capturing machine from show services. This is an easy and sophisticated way to obtain attendee information. Your list of prospects will become a valuable database and marketing tool for the future. The wise sales manager will establish written quotas for the sales team and offer incentives and a reward system to motivate the staff toward collecting a higher number of qualified leads.

At a tradeshow most attendees will have business cards to drop into a bowl. Writing notes on the back of the business card works fine in the U.S., but remember that it will be viewed as an insult in Europe or Asia. Other options are to design a lead slip or survey card for gathering contact information. This is especially important for exhibitors selling at a consumer show. A lead slip is better than a business card because you can include a few questions that help you qualify the lead and determine what product or service is desired, when the prospect plans to buy, budget considerations and how and when to follow up with them. At the bottom of your lead slip leave a place for the staff member's initials and develop a code to identify what leads came from which show. This will help when tracking the lead's value and will help identify the most productive shows. If you use the lead slip approach instead of taking business cards, then place the lead slip on a clipboard and require staff to approach prospects to gather the information. Leaving the slips on the table expecting anyone to pick them up and fill them out will leave you disappointed.

After you acquire a lead, go one step further than your competitor probably will and rank the lead. A simple ranking system will help evaluate and prioritize the leads. Your ranking system can be as simple as ABC. On the back of the lead slip, survey sheet or business card, mark a letter "A" for any prospect that has an immediate need. "B" leads will be those that will probably buy within six to twelve months warranting regular follow up, while a "C" lead is not a good lead and probably just wanted your promotional products.

Lead follow-up traditionally happens in the days following the close of a show, although there are some exhibitors who actually fax or email leads back to the office each day for immediate follow up. If you are not one of those companies, then you may not be looking at those leads for several days, maybe even a week. You will never remember the conversation you had with the prospect by the time you get around to making the contact. The leads may also be distributed to other staff members, office help or sales representatives in other departments for follow-up. If you are gathering business cards or your lead slip doesn't offer all the answers to your important questions, just jot down a note on the back about the conversation you had. What question did the customer want answered? What product or service are they interested in? What information do you need to get back to them? If you add a personal comment it will help to jog the person's memory about what was discussed. Write a note that they were from your home-town, talked about the local sports team or just had a baby. This reference, along with the sales dialog, will make the call more personal even when you are not doing the follow-up yourself.

If you prepare beforehand you might be able to skip the follow-up altogether. When you can't close the sale on the spot you can increase your chances for a post-show sale by scheduling an appointment for a future sales call, booking an in-home demonstration, an office presentation, or consultation right then and there. Be ready to respond quickly by having your appointment book and calendar handy. Review the sample lead form included here and select the areas that meet your needs.

Lead management

It is important to remember to put someone in charge of your leads. Exhibit Experts offers exhibits for rent as well as for sale. On more than one occasion, the rental display has returned from a show with the client's lead box and leads inside. Bill thought Mary had them. Mary thought John had them. The truth is, I had them and they didn't even know it. To prevent this from happening to your company, consider these questions. What is your plan for the leads? Will each sales person be responsible for holding onto the leads they personally collect or will the leads be turned in daily to a designated person? Will the leads be distributed randomly to the sales staff or assigned to certain sales territories? Before

the show determine where the leads will be stored ar
one person to take them out of the booth nightly. Another
option is to ask each staff person to be personally responsible
for the leads they collect. Some companies prefer to review
the leads nightly and fax or express mail the best ones back to
the office for immediate follow-up. Regardless of which plan
you choose, be sure to take care of those valuable contacts.

LEAD FORM

Ranking (circle one) A B C Show name _____

Salesperson _____ Date _____

Name _____

Company _____

Phone number _____

E-mail _____

Address _____

City, State, Zip _____

Product of interest _____

Time frame to purchase _____

Personal note _____

_____

Decision maker   Y N   Influencer   Y N

Time frame to buy   3-6 mo.   6-12 mo.

Follow up action _____

_____

Date/time to call _____Appointment set _____

Product of interest _____

#3 – Investigate the competition

To improve your products, services, sales and profits, it's important to learn all you can about your competition. Competitive intelligence is neither illegal nor unethical. It is your responsibility to be knowledgeable of other offerings like yours in order to educate the buyer and prevent any misrepresentations. Don't miss the chance to investigate your competitor's exhibit, product offerings and staff behaviors.

The attendees will be comparing competing products so you should too. If you know the staff of the competing company simply stop by for a quick chat about business in general or the state of the industry. If you are not familiar with the company, take off your ID badge and walk to the competitor's display area. Without entering the exhibit, observe the activity inside the booth and determine what they're doing right, as well as what they're doing wrong. Watch the staff and listen to their sales presentation, check out the product line, pricing and packaging. Are new products or services being introduced? How effective are the display and marketing materials? How do your exhibit and materials compare? How do customers react to their exhibit? Observe the behavior of the staff. What are they doing to attract customers? If their employee approaches you, simply introduce yourself and identify your company. Say hello and mention where your booth is, then quickly make your exit. Make notes about the information you gather and hold a meeting after the show to relate and share this information with the entire sales team. The objective is not to be deceptive, but to gain knowledge.

#4 – Gather market research

It is not unusual for large companies to spend enormous amounts of money on market research that will shape the direction of the sales and marketing departments. While you are at your booth you have a million dollar opportunity to check the pulse of the public. It is your chance to ask the hard questions of potential purchasers. The show can serve as your own private focus group. With a well-planned questionnaire you can acquire valuable demographical information. You can take a survey and ask your target audience what they really want from a business like yours. What issues are important to them, what makes them angry, what gets them excited, what would they change and what could be done better? This is the perfect way to find out what people really think about your company and staff.

Provide an opportunity for them to rate your services on a scale of one to ten. What is their opinion of your business services and products? What do they think of the style, color, variety, pricing, speed of delivery or courtesy of the staff? Take this opportunity to find out what bothers them and what they like best so you can address their needs in the most beneficial way. Doing so will help you build your company's strengths as well as eliminate weaknesses, as seen through the eyes of your customers.

#5 – Network with exhibitors

A well-trained exhibit staff will make good use of the valuable networking opportunities they will have with attendees at every event. Few, however, take advantage of the opportunity to network with the other exhibitors. Every exhibitor at the show can be an important resource for your company. Take a walk around the show floor and stop by each booth for a visit. Introduce yourself and ask them which shows were successful for their company and what new events or selling opportunities are they aware of that might fit your customer profile. Share information about new products, suppliers, packaging, business services or display ideas. By meeting all the other exhibitors you can uncover valuable information that could reduce trade show expenses and enhance your business operations. Make it a point to take time before, during and after an event to meet and chat with as many vendors as possible. In many cases there are a limited number of exhibit staffers on hand and they are often cloistered in their own booth space with no time to get around to visiting other companies. They are also an untapped source of sales for you. With this knowledge you can prepare a plan ahead of time to turn them into customers. Create a sales flyer with a show special just for them. Offer a discount or other incentive to encourage sales before show's end. Don't forget to network with attendees too. Attend all the breakfasts, roundtables, mixers, seminars and group events offered during the show and use these opportunities to connect with all participants involved.

#6 – Build your company image

In one season your company and products can be seen by thousands of people who attend shows. Your participation can be an excellent way to build credibility and reinforce name recognition for your company. Don't hesitate to show off your company spirit and brag a little. Here are some ways of taking the greatest advantage of this opportunity. If you have received publicity that appeared in a newspaper or magazine, awards for your work, special certifications, written client testimonials or impressive letters of recommendation from satisfied clients or vendors, be sure to display these at your booth or hand out copies in flyer form. If you sponsor a charity, serve on a special committee or belong to a prestigious organization, let your customers know about it. One vendor at the International Sportsmen's Expo had several photos of her grandson with his 4H projects and awards. Another exhibitor proudly displayed his membership in the wildlife conservation organization, Ducks Unlimited. Those connections struck a cord with attendees and initiated dialog.

Put up a picture of the owners or your management team. Select your friendliest sales staff to work in the booth. Remember, all things being equal, customers buy from people they like and people they enjoy doing business with. Try to uncover common bonds between your product, your sales staff and your prospects. This will build valuable buyer loyalty and generate more sales.

A great example comes from a client who is a financial planner. At every show he puts a framed picture of his wife, himself and his Labrador retriever on the counter in his booth. Within minutes someone is asking about the picture, discussing labradors, and opening up a dialog with his client that gradually turns to financial planning. The key is to find a common interest that initiates a friendly conversation.

#7 – Recruit personnel

Do you need extra employees during your busy season? Does your company wish to expand the sales staff, find new manufacturers' representatives, build a bigger down line or increase your dealer or distributor base? As you talk to people throughout the show, keep a lookout for individuals who have the personality and skills needed to fill those jobs. Keep job applications handy so you can obtain their employment information at the show. This not only gives you a chance to interview on the spot, but it saves you the cost of advertising for help in the future.

#8 – Feature something new

One of the primary reasons anyone goes to trade shows is to look for new products and industry innovations. You can capitalize on this knowledge by launching a new product line or introducing a special service at the show. When you debut the new line why not launch it with fanfare and create an attraction to build excitement at your booth. For example, incorporate a publicity stunt or promotional theme designed to gain media attention that would attract a reporter to your booth. Put the item on a revolving pedestal or cover it up and only reveal it at set intervals throughout each day of the show. Hold a contest to name the new line or product. If you want to keep a lower profile or just test market prototypes, solicit the opinions of the attendees at the show and use the research to evaluate the investment.

#9 – Introduce important people

Customers rarely get a chance to meet or speak to the principals or decision makers of a company. It makes a memorable impression when the CEO, president, manager or owner of the business takes the time to make themselves available to the attendees at a trade show. This technique works just as well with the chef, inventor, artist, tour guide or author at a public show.

Make sure the guest of honor stands out from the other staff members. Have them wear the company ball cap, a brightly colored scarf or a designer tie. Have them put on a special nametag that identifies them in a unique way. The owner of a cheesecake company wears a button that reads "The Big Cheese." A retailer of various beef and turkey jerky products tags himself as "The Jerky Guy."

Give them a spot of honor in the display area. Walk clients over and introduce them to the special person. Let them shake hands, mingle and answer questions. Another option is to schedule five minute, one-on-one conferences at the booth so they can have a private chat with visitors.

Be sure to have someone run interference so no one ties the VIP up too long or uses the time to complain. It may take some creative scheduling, but if you can manage to let customers get up close and personal with the decision makers, you will be perceived as a company genuinely interested in the customer's needs. That builds valuable credibility in the marketplace, makes a lasting and memorable impression on attendees and provides a beneficial competitive edge.

#10–Prepare to get publicity

Having a camera crew from a news station surround your booth while a reporter interviews you on site is a guaranteed way to draw attention to your exhibit. This could happen to you if you plan and prepare ahead of time. Let the media know of your plans. Go on the internet or look in the yellow pages of the city you will be exhibiting in. Compile a list of the local media contacts. Send out 20 press releases to newspapers, radio and TV outlets prior to the show. Reporters have a lot of newspaper space and TV time to fill and are hungry for interesting stories and people to feature. Create a newsworthy angle that would pique their interest. The information must be of value to their specific audience, the attendees or the community at large. Reporters want stories that educate, enlighten, amuse, entertain and inform their audiences. Always present your story as important information for the public. Never overtly promote your products or services as if you were trying to sell them. Here are several hooks or angles that would capture a TV or news reporter's attention. If your company hired a superstar, broke a record, staged an unusual demonstration, brought in a celebrity, hosted a seminar, received an award, unveiled a new product, promoted a charity or celebrated a company milestone, then you have an appealing angle for the press. Prepare to announce it and flaunt it. If you take time to position yourself right with a catchy angle and headline you could receive thousands of dollars worth of free publicity.

Taking the time and effort to develop the right publicity angle could land you on the 6:00 news or tomorrow's front page. Be proactive and go after exposure for your company, products and services. Many events provide various ways for reporters to tap into great stories about the exhibitors. Get into the new product showcase if you qualify and one is available. Write an article or provide information in the show daily where the media look for points of interest. Look for journalists and reporters on the floor and be prepared to wow them with a great idea. Have a press kit or demo CD prepared and ready when the opportunity presents itself. If you have something outstanding to announce, call a press conference.

When your efforts pay off and you receive your picture and news story on the front page of the business section be prepared to exploit it to your advantage. Collect as many copies of the publication as you can. Save the front masthead of the paper or magazine. Cut and paste the article with the masthead and publication date at the top. Laminate, dry mount or frame it and display it at your booth during your next show. Make a collage of the various articles you receive. Make reprints of all articles and pass them out at all your shows and networking events. Print a list of the dates and locations of your next five exhibiting events on the bottom of the reprints. On the backside place an advertisement and special incentive offer for your company and products to encourage sales.

#11 – Connect with existing customers

Many attendees go to the same shows year after year. The chances are good that you will run into some of your best clients and customers at a trade show or public show. Use this knowledge to capitalize on the opportunity to connect with them and thank them for their business. Compile a list of your top 50 clients and send out a pre-show mailer inviting them to your booth. Prepare your staff with the names and business details of those customers most likely to attend. Look at the name badges of attendees passing by your booth and call out to those customers you recognize and greet them with confidence. They will be thoroughly impressed when you call them by name and reward them with a nice gift. Don't miss this wonderful way to strengthen existing client relationships and reinforce customer loyalty.

Put it into action

Give serious consideration to each of these ideas and try to implement three or more into your marketing plan. Create a goal sheet for each employee that must be filled out at the end of each show day. Require your staff to collect a specific number of leads or fill out a certain number of survey cards. Ask them for one or two observations about the competition, and a suggestion for a future show. Make your employees accountable for specific productivity and reward them for their efforts with gifts for the most productive members of the team. By giving the staff specific objectives such as gathering information about the competition, looking for unique marketing and display ideas, new supplier contacts, and qualified leads, you guarantee that even if the sales fall short of expectations, your business will benefit from the valuable information gathered by the staff.

SHOW GOAL SHEET

Date _____

Name of Show_____

Staff Member _____

Show Assignment	**Actual Results**
Collect _____ qualified leads	_____
Perform _____ product demonstrations	_____
Fill out _____ survey cards	_____
Visit _____ competitors exhibits	_____
Make _____ appointments for sales calls	_____
Find _____ creative display ideas	_____
Interview _____ potential distributors	_____
Give away _____ corporate gifts	_____
Obtain _____ buyers' business cards	_____

Create a
Dynamic Display

Image is everything on the show floor

Every exhibitor will be seen by thousands of people during a show season. They will be your employees, management, competitors, customers and industry leaders. Many will be qualified prospects, but many more will know someone who needs what you have to offer. How the public perceives you and your company at the show has tremendous impact on your credibility and whether they will refer business or do business with you or not.

I recently attended a local Home Show at the Phoenix Convention Center. A well-known financial planning and investment firm was exhibiting and approached me about my investment needs. Here was a billion dollar company responsible to millions of investors, claiming to offer expertise that would make my money grow. As the salesman talked, I glanced around his exhibit. He had the smallest of show spaces. His vinyl banner was falling down behind him. His table created an uninviting barrier across the front of his booth space. Hand lettered signs were taped to a glass bowl. Piles of brochures were carelessly spread across the tabletop. His associate sat behind the table snacking. Another was on the cell phone. What is wrong with this picture?

My first impression was that the company didn't have enough money to make a professional presentation at the show and didn't care enough to want to impress me, so why would I think they could handle my investments in a competent manner. My perception of them at the show didn't match the polished image they portrayed in their corporate brochure. In my eyes, they had no credibility.

An impressive display is critical to your exhibit marketing success. It should create interest, attract attention and lure the prospect to the booth so the sales staff can initiate a conversation in order to qualify the buyer, obtain a lead, or make a sale. What is so exciting about this venue for self-promotion and selling is that the exhibit floor is a level playing field for any kind of business. Each exhibitor, no matter how big or small, has equal exposure and access to the same qualified prospects. With a little creativity, time and attention to detail, even a small home-based business can craft a powerful presence that captures just as much attention as the Fortune 500 Company in the booth next door.

The savvy business owner will capitalize on this important knowledge. The next time you plan to exhibit in a tradeshow, sell your products in a consumer show, sponsor an event or give a seminar, think about how you will be perceived by the audience. Plan your presentation carefully. Take time to make sure the image your audience sees matches the professionalism in your brochure, the hype in your advertising and the promises touted by your staff. At a tradeshow, perception is powerful and image is everything.

Your display is your traveling store, your mobile business, your recruiting station, your portable office or your personal marketing tool. At a glance it must tell people who you are, what you do and why they should want to do business with you. In the distracting atmosphere of a show, time is your biggest competitor. On the crowded, noisy show floor you have only about seven seconds to capture the customer's attention. That's about the time it takes to stroll past the first ten feet of booth space. For this reason, you need an attractive, unusual or eye-catching display that will not only get noticed, but will be remembered long after the show is over.

Think back to the last time you walked the floor of a major trade show or consumer marketplace. You probably passed by hundreds of displays that looked pretty uninteresting. Then, suddenly something unique caught your eye. What made you stop, look and remember? It could have been a clever sign, eye-catching props, attractive colors, unusual decorations, beautiful graphics, an interactive game or demonstration that grabbed your attention. It might have been because of something the staff was wearing or doing.

There are three elements involved in creating a dynamic display. They are: the display hardware, the merchandising method and the marketing message. These elements must work together to communicate your ideas and reinforce your image effectively. Don't look at these elements in a disjointed way when designing your selling and marketing environment. It is not about each individual element, but rather the way they coordinate together in a seamless, cohesive fashion to create an atmosphere of excitement and an environment of energy, warmth, color, competence and professionalism that will draw customers in.

Your display will have a huge impact on your company image, and it must also be practical. The design should be driven by your needs and desire to accomplish the maximum return on investment. Therefore, before we discuss each of the design elements in detail, your first order of business must be to determine the goals you want to accomplish at the show and the needs of your sales staff. Decide, in advance of looking at display designs, what you must have in the booth to facilitate the salespeople to accomplish those goals. Will you require demonstration counters to debut a new product? Do you need plenty of storage and display areas to hold products you will be retailing? Is a conference room necessary? Where will the computers be positioned? How will the electrical services be run? How do you want the attendees to flow through the display?

Secondly, get a clear picture of the dimensions of the booth space you have purchased. Too often a company has an inflated perception of how much floor space they actually have and overestimate how much they can realistically fit into that space. Get some perspective on the size of your space by taping out the dimensions on the floor in your office or use grid paper to keep your early planning in perspective.

Most importantly, bring the salespeople who will be working at the booth together with the marketing team to brainstorm the plan and design together. Expensive mistakes and design blunders are commonly made when the marketing department is left to create a grandiose structure that might look spectacular but delivers inadequate space and tools that the sales staff requires to do their job. To assure that the best possible display structure is purchased and the most effective marketing messages are designed make sure the sales and marketing departments are communicating together through the entire process.

Design around a theme

If you want your exhibit to have maximum imp
element of your display should come together in a
harmonizing manner. Studies show that themed exhibits draw
more traffic and register higher audience recall than those
without themes. The theme should create a mood, have a
focus or tell a story in a way that will attract your target
audience. It should be familiar and easily understood by
prospects and customers. Most importantly, the theme should
create excitement, stimulate an emotion, and project the
company's sense of humor, professionalism and personality.
The key to an effective theme is creativity and making sure it
is appropriate for your products and services.

 The theme's purpose is to capture attention and reinforce
your sales message. Your display theme can revolve around
your product, service, advertising message, slogan or tag line.
You can work with a company mascot, a current event or
trend, a popular movie, sport, catchy song, a holiday, the selling
season or simply tie into the theme that the promoter has
picked for the show.

You can evoke emotions with a theme such as romance or
relaxation. Ideas for clever themes are everywhere. Jungle
themes, sports themes, Hollywood themes, gambling themes
and '50s cafe themes are just a few of the most popular ones.
Set up a committee to brainstorm an idea that will suit your
goals and help promote the message you wish to give your
audience. Coordinate everything from the display fixtures,
props, graphics, signs and advertising, to the staff attire and
free give-aways so they work together to enhance the
marketing message. If done properly, a coordinated display
with a creative theme will not only increase traffic to your
booth, but will make a strong impression on the attendees

that will be remembered and talked about long after the show has concluded.

Integrate interesting props

One very effective way to add interest and excitement to your display is to incorporate props in your booth to compliment your theme. The right props will grab the attention of passersby, help illustrate intangible services and make your products more appealing. Use props to elevate your products and literature so they are closer to eye level. Select props that will enhance your theme, drive home your message, stimulate an emotion and bring your products or service to life.

Service businesses particularly benefit from the use of props to accent their display themes. With no physical product at hand, these companies need a way to illustrate their intangible services. Making use of the mini-vignette will help. This entails creating a little scene with products and props that will help the customer visualize your point. For example, financial planners selling college savings programs would use props consisting of graduation photos, a cap and gown and a diploma. A travel agent promoting trips to Mexico could cover their table with Mexican blankets and decorate with a sombrero, bright fabric, confetti and woven baskets. Use a small suitcase covered with the Mexican flag and travel stickers as the lead container. A popular sandwich shop called Paradise Bakery that specializes in healthy sandwiches and delicious cookies and muffins was exhibiting in a tradeshow with a beach theme. They put a large beach umbrella in the center of the booth and covered the base with a beach towel. Tables lined the perimeter of the space. Each was covered with brightly colored beach towels, some sand, sand toys, plastic buckets, shovels, sunglasses, visors and tanning lotion.

The buckets and toys were filled with assorted muffins and cookies and the front table was set with a picnic lunch complete with pitcher of ice tea. Attendees were encouraged to walk through the booth to sample the goodies.

Help your customers envision a reason to buy. A boat company exhibiting at a sportsmen's expo had an impressive assortment of fabulous boats on display in a huge space, but not one prop in the entire display. Think for a moment why most people buy boats. The want to go fishing and throw parties! I suggested that they fill a few of the boats with balloons, place several colorful ice coolers filled with refreshments on deck and add several fishing rods at the end of the boat complete with huge fish on the hooks. Complete the scene by running a string of bikinis up the flagpole. That's the boating experience most people would love to have. And if they can envision it they are more likely to buy it.

The vignette approach draws attention and helps the browser identify, at a glance, what the exhibitor is offering much better than stacks of brochures on a table. Simply adding inexpensive flowers and plants can dress up a display setting. They come in handy for concealing electrical wiring and they add a nice touch to the booth environment. The key to successful, memorable merchandising is to incorporate props and products into attractive focal points that will complement the theme and grab your customer's attention. Consider the following types of props and how they might be incorporated into your display.

Bigger is better

Giant props can add pizzazz to a booth. They are guaranteed to draw attention to your company and are both fun and memorable. Enlarge your best selling product, your company mascot or something that helps to illustrate your service. A nationwide exterminating company brings a giant remote controlled roach to each show. The salespeople let it roam around the floor in front of their display. It's ugly and gross, but extremely effective in grabbing the attention of show attendees. A national coffee company uses a giant cup of coffee complete with steam from dry ice to create excitement. One dentist has a four-foot toothbrush and a six-foot tube of toothpaste in his booth to make people smile and stop in. A printing service enlarges its business card and letterhead and uses it as an eye-catching backdrop. Boldness and creativity are sure to capture the attention of passersby. Give some thought to what you can enlarge and display as a giant point of interest.

It's a small world

Miniature props can have just as much of an impact as giant props. In addition to drawing in the curious, they can help you to display a product too cumbersome to transport to the show. Miniature working models of your product, your company vehicle or replicas of your warehouse or storefront are items that would make impressive miniature props. A drilling company displays a perfectly detailed model of their drilling rig, while a power company displays an entire miniature construction site complete with dirt hills and construction vehicles. A moving company brings their one-third scale moving van to the show and uses the trailer end as their counter. Everything from jet engines to full size automobiles can be reduced to small working models saving not only space, but freight costs as well.

Expand your space

A very unique way to utilize your exhibit space is to integrate props and products throughout your entire booth. Look at your space as one cohesive showcase. One example comes from a company selling cookware and kitchen gadgets that turned their booth into a gourmet kitchen. They brought in a counter, stove and sink and used large attractive graphic murals of a kitchen to create depth in the booth. They decorated the area with appliances, utensils and other coordinating props so it looked just like someone's kitchen in a beautiful home and merchandised their products throughout. Don't be afraid to stretch your imagination for clever ideas.

An office supply company might create the perfect workspace in their booth by bringing in an elegant desk, comfortable chair, wood grain filing cabinet and bookshelf. Then, decorate the entire area with all the accessories that would make it desirable to any executive or home-based entrepreneur.

An award-winning example of this technique was used effectively by a local Arizona bank. A display was constructed to look like the lobby of a branch of the bank that was pictured in a photo from the late 1800s. The lobby consisted of mahogany counters, a wall safe and teller cages complete with a teller in a handle-bar mustache. It was designed to fit entirely inside a 10' x 10' in-line booth space, yet when you entered you felt like you were in a bank not a display. This attention grabbing display provided an effective atmosphere in which to promote the bank's services, while underscoring their long-time commitment to the community.

Upscale furniture stores use this technique of integrated merchandising very successfully. They don't pile sofas in one room, chairs in another and tables in yet another area. They create complete room settings that paint a beautiful picture of how their furniture would look in your home. They present the master bedroom or den of your dreams, with every detail in place, and every accessory included, ready for you to purchase. This effective merchandising method offers a way to display your product or service in a setting that will create an appealing buying atmosphere for the customer.

Magnetic merchandising

Merchandising is the way you decorate your booth and present your products and services to the public. You can impact an attendee emotionally by how you merchandise your display. It can have an industrial feel, a commercial look, be warm and inviting or hip and contemporary depending on your use of color, fixtures, textures and props. How you display your offerings has a great impact on your company image and shapes the impression you make on the prospects at a trade or consumer show. It's surprising how many companies believe that stringing up a banner, setting stacks of flyers on a table and piles of product on a shelf is a sufficient presentation to attract qualified customers.

Think about how you would perceive such a display. Does your company's exhibit exemplify the type of image you wish to convey to the public? Do your offerings look as good on the show floor as they do in your store, office or showroom? Does your product display look as good or better than your competitor's? If the image you convey at your exhibit is not equal to the personality, degree of professionalism and quality represented in your company brochures and advertising, you will lose credibility with prospects and customers at the show.

There are many merchandising ideas that can help you create a more integrated display that is both professional and dynamic. Many exhibitors make the mistake of filling their booth with too much product. They are under the impression they must bring everything the company sells or prospects may not see what they want and pass by without stopping.

Regardless of whether you're permitted to sell at the show or not, your display will be much more attractive and appealing if you select a few representative samples of inventory or only display the best sellers in the line. Put the excess stock out of sight so your booth is neat, organized and uncluttered. You can, however, show the depth of your product line using software presentations, interactive product catalogs, a video tour of your store, a catalog or photo portfolio of your goods.

If you are retailing products at a consumer show consider this tip. If you constantly fill up your racks or shelves with more products every time you sell a unit, it will look as if you are never selling anything. When you sell something, leave the space empty so it gives the impression that what you have is in demand and the customer better grab one now before they are all gone.

Dress up the staff

A clever way to get your company noticed is to carry the marketing theme through to the staff's wardrobe. Request that each employee wear a costume or outfit that adds some flare or helps exemplify your marketing message. A bank using the theme "It's a jungle out there," decorated the back wall of their display with a photomural depicting a lush tropical jungle with animals all about. The front tables were covered with grass cloth. While steel drums played in the background, employees wearing khaki safari outfits, Indiana Jones hats and binoculars around their necks greeted attendees. A travel agent promoting Hawaiian cruises had employees wear brightly colored tropical shirts, coordinated shorts and flower leis. A doctor who invented an ergonomic computer keyboard attended the show with his wife to launch the product. He wore a smart suit with a purple custom necktie and she wore a matching scarf. The fabric colors worked with the color scheme of the display and they both stood out in distinctive style. Most trade shows tend to have a business-like atmosphere where everyone is in conservative attire. If you want to maintain a professional look, yet still stand out in the crowd, consider letting your employees wear matching polo shirts or sweaters with the company logo. Change the style or color of the shirt each day. If your company has a recognizable uniform, have the booth staff wear it to reinforce your image. Consider dressing in a manner that that will help customers to differentiate your employees from the attendees standing in your booth. Remember to keep clothing comfortable, since trade show days are often long and exhausting. Don't be too conservative! Get creative and add an element of fun.

Grab them with graphics

A very critical element of a dynamic display is the presentation of your marketing and sales messages. Graphics are the pictures and words on your display and contribute much to an attendee's first impression of your company's professionalism, personality and product benefits. At a glance, attendees must understand who you are, what you do and why they need you. The audience passes by your display so quickly they have very little time to absorb your message. Remember, the primary purpose of your display is to catch the customer's attention causing them to pause long enough for your sales staff to engage them in a conversation. Great graphics pique prospects' interest and compel them to stop and ask questions.

Keep text to a minimum

Avoid wordy messages on your display. A common mistake many exhibitors make is trying to tell too much. Keep all statements short, succinct and simple to read. Only ten percent of passers-by will read or remember your written words. Limit your messages to three or four main ideas that summarize each point in eight words or less. Stay away from teeny tiny text. Make sure you can easily read your graphics from 10' away. Promote your company slogan or advertising tag line to enhance branding. Always emphasize benefits over features. Telling the audience how you can solve their most critical problems is more important than listing what you do or telling how great you think you are. A feature tells the audience what you do, while a benefit tells them what you do for them. When you plan your sales message think about how an effective newspaper headline grabs the reader's attention and entices them to read more. Many companies insist on splashing their name and logo all over the display. It is important to identify your company in the booth, but unless yours is a highly recognized brand, you would be better served by trying a more intriguing approach. When you create your next set of graphics, consider using a funny headline on your header. Ask a question, share a statistic or make a bold statement that creates interest and piques curiosity.

Go for the WOW factor

If you want to increase an attendee's retention of your marketing message, then place the words over large, attractive, colorful, eye-catching pictures. Thirty-five percent of the attendees will remember more of your message when it is incorporated into an interesting picture. Big, bold murals and large-format graphics make a much more impressive impact on the audience, and will capture their attention quicker than a series of small images. Use interesting photographs, creative drawings, or colorful illustrations that show your product in use or your staff helping customers.

A company that sells slip proof flooring mats to restaurants used a highly effective graphic to illustrate the need for their product. The photo was of a waitress carrying a serving tray loaded with plates of food skidding backwards and about to fall on a slippery floor. The text simply read "With Slip Free Floor Mats this will never happen to you."

You can use pictures to transport visitors through the manufacturing process. Customer testimonials are very effective on the booth. Take an impressive testimonial from a client and composite it over their picture and logo. Consider using images that create an emotional connection, make the message memorable and urge the audience to act. Repetition is a proven principle of effective advertising. You will get more mileage from your messages if you integrate all marketing and sales efforts together. Make sure your tradeshow graphics repeat the most important sales messages and images found in your current advertising campaign, brochures and sales sheets, and on your website. Threading that same message and method through your pre-show mailings, handouts and follow-up materials will reinforce it, brand your company and help the customer remember who you are long after the show ends.

Think off-the-wall

An economical way to add pizzazz to your display is to use some cut-to-shape graphics. By extending your graphics beyond the geometric lines of your exhibit walls, you can add a 3-D element that will be unique and eye-catching. An ~ance company's mural graphics featured a group of ~ning in the park while carrying a bouquet of top of each balloon in the picture was cut nat they looked more realistic. The balloons ust above the top wall of the display and appeared

57

to be floating. That simple, inexpensive treatment added enormous visual impact to the entire display.

Another trick is to use a cut-to-shape image that appears to be coming out of the background graphic. A gun dealer had a 20' graphic mural of a lush, green forest. Instead of incorporating pictures of animals in the mural, he used cut outs of a large grizzly bear and a ten-point buck. He added 4' blocks of foam core to the backs of the pictures and attached them to the mural. The bear and buck extended out from the forest image adding amazing depth and realism to the display. A wine bar had a beautiful wide-angle picture of a wine cellar on their 20' display wall. They placed attractive wine racks filled with bottles of wine and glasses against the displays. They enhanced the visual impact by using wine barrels as counters. The wine cellar seemed to come alive as it extended out into the display area.

Many companies want to incorporate large graphic images into their display, but their product line changes often requiring the need to replace old products with new product pictures. Large graphics are costly to print, but smaller, more economical graphics do not have the same visual impact. There are several solutions to this dilemma. Print large graphic murals that will represent the corporate image to any audience, then add smaller, individual pictures or copy panels around it that address the specific audiences or each different show. Another option is to print a large graphic wall and leave empty areas within the large images so you can attach smaller graphic panels then change them out as needed.

Use key colors

Color will add drama to your display. Give careful consideration to the colors you will use when designing your exhibit. Select a color scheme that is consistent with your business image. The colors that are found in your logo, company letterhead or product packaging should be incorporated into your presentation to reinforce your business identity. You can add interest by contrasting the fabric or laminate colors on your display. For creative effect, reverse out the colors in your graphics using dark backgrounds with light lettering instead of light backgrounds with dark lettering. Use specific colors that reflect something about your industry that might draw attention to your booth. For example, if you are a manufacturer's representative for a line of children's toys you might use bold primary colors to project a playful atmosphere in your booth. A mortgage company might accent their booth with the color green for money. A conservative bank might use gray or black color combinations. Going totally monochromatic will encourage a second look. Color-coordinate every aspect of your display to enhance your theme or company colors. Make the entire booth presentation cohesive by repeating the colors in your props, graphics, literature, table covers and advertising.

Certain colors stimulate the brain and are proven to affect a person's mood. Here some colors and their associations:

Green – Nature	Black – Authority
Red – Excitement	Yellow – Optimism
White – Purity	Blue – Serenity

Create compelling graphics

Your graphic images are only as good as the artwork from which they are created. If you do not possess graphic design knowledge, this will be a very difficult concept to grasp. In this age of the digital camera, everyone assumes that the gorgeous photograph they took of the sunset over the ocean or the shot of the company warehouse can be enlarged and used as a 10' background picture on their exhibit. People think that their elaborate website images or pictures from their brochure can be reproduced for use as their display artwork. There is a huge learning curve associated with understanding how digital graphics are designed. The simple truth is, unless you have pictures, logos, fonts or illustrations originally created in a format that can be digitally manipulated, you will not be able to turn a 3" x 4" picture from your brochure into a 6' mural for your tradeshow booth. There a something called DPI, (dots per inch), that determines whether your artwork will look like a crisp, beautiful picture or a blurry, jagged mess. To ensure perfection, the images you select for use on your display should be designed in Adobe Illustrator, Photoshop or other graphic design program by someone who understands that your goal is to enlarge them for tradeshow use.

In addition, it is important to respect the time and talent it takes for a graphic designer to sit at a computer and create, size, format, crop, edit, composite, assemble, layout and finish all the elements of your artwork to make it ready for print. The clock starts ticking the moment a designer sits at the computer, so brainstorm with your sales and marketing teams and get recommendations from your exhibit company about what images and messages will create the greatest impact for your company at the show, before handing everything over to the designer. An experienced, competent exhibit company can save you a lot of money by providing free consultation and assistance with conceptualizing your marketing message and display design. Your display consultant should offer expertise and insight into what will give you the greatest return on your investment. The cost of your designs many seem expensive, with average design fees at $125 per hour, but remember, you will own them and can use them later on your website, flyers, brochures and advertising.

Producing graphics

When your graphic designs are completed, burned to a CD, uploaded to the FTP site of the production house and ready to produce, you have a variety of options for printing and mounting. This is the digital age, so most tradeshow graphics are no longer produced photographically with chemicals, but are translated from a computer program to the large format printer and onto your substrate. The quality of printing will vary greatly. Like the display itself, you have many choices in quality and cost. If you want quality products that will withstand long-term use and present a crisp, bright, professional look for your company, go with a print house that offers high quality ink jet or Lambda print technology. Today's contemporary displays can support a variety of graphic treatments. Your images can be directly printed onto fabric, mesh, vinyl or acrylic. They can be mounted onto foam core or gatorboard, although these are not recommended for the rigorous demands of tradeshow use. Large format murals for tradeshow exhibits are commonly printed onto a polycarbonate or paper, laminated on the front with a clear plastic, then a thinner laminate is placed on the backside sandwiching your pictures in between. The process can use hot or cold mounting technology to create a durable, brilliantly colored, photograph, collage, text panel, logo or any image you desire.

Cost-saving tips for graphics

Taking proper care of your graphics will keep them looking beautiful for years. The cost of your graphics will be roughly one-third to one-half the cost of your exhibit, so care should be taken to ensure they are safe and intact for every show. Invest in durable shipping containers. Consider storing graphics separately from the display hardware to prevent damage. Ask your exhibit company to provide you with instructions on how to care for your graphics. Can you roll them or must they be transported or stored flat? Do you roll them image in or image out? How do you clean them? What temperature restrictions are there for storing your graphics? How long can they be stored in their container without effecting their condition or shape? Knowing the answers to these questions will help you extend the life of your artwork.

Prevent graphic nightmares

There are many opportunities for things to go wrong from the time your display and graphics get shipped from your office to the time they arrive at your booth for set up. To prevent an exhibitor's nightmare, always bring a CD containing all your tradeshow graphics with you to the show. If your graphics get lost or damaged you will be prepared to replace them. The convention services company will be able to connect you with a local graphic production house or if you need them in a hurry you can rush off to the local quick printer. Either way, you will look like a hero for saving the day and the show.

Table covers

When you are working with six or eight foot draped tables in your booth the fabric colors provided by the convention services company are not always colors that work well with your display and graphics. Consider purchasing custom made table covers in your company colors. Your logo or marketing message or full color artwork can be imprinted, embroidered or appliqued onto the fabric to add continuity and personalization to your display.

Turn on the lights

Statistics prove that lights attract attention to an exhibit. You can use lighting in a variety of ways to enhance your booth. Neon, chase lights, flashers, LED lights or strobes will capture attention. Colored bulbs, light filters and fiber optic lighting can be used to create a special mood. Other options include light boxes, backlighting some of your graphic images and spot lighting to accent products or service messages. You can never predict what the lighting conditions will be like from one exhibit hall to the next, so be prepared to illuminate your display, if needed. The low voltage bulbs are the most popular and save on power. Electricity for lighting in your booth will cost an extra $50 or more above the booth fee. Consult your exhibitor packet for electrical hook-up restrictions on certain types of lighting and charges. The added expense will be justified by the practical applications and added drama that specialty lighting will give your exhibit.

Technology and tricks

In this age of technology you have an endless choice of unique applications for tradeshow use. There are simple, inexpensive options like the wiggling table or a rotating turntable on which to display products. There are waterfalls that can spell out your logo, holograms that change messages from various angles, three-dimensional graphics, projection methods to create talking heads in a box, images on the floor and floating products. Using motion to attract attention can be accomplished with something as simple as a 60-second loop video on a laptop or a slide show. More sophisticated options would be a video wall or projections of color or images onto walls, floors or ceilings. There is no limit to the creativity that can be achieved with the right budget.

EXHIBIT Li

Give your display the critical eye

Before you attend the next show, set up your di?
the staff to take a critical look at it. Walk past at differen
angles as an attendee would. Take photos of the completed
display noting positions of graphics, products and accessories,
as a record of reference. A copy of the display will come in
handy for the installation crew. I am often asked to serve as a
booth judge by the show promoter who wants to award
prizes to exhibiting business based on my evaluation. Awards
are usually given for most creative decor, best merchandising,
best use of theme and best overall design. The following
criteria used in the judging process, are valued at 1-5 points
each. These can serve as a simple checklist with which you can
evaluate your own company's exhibit.

- ❑ Can you tell at a glance who the company is and what
  they do?

- ❑ Is the sales or marketing message immediately clear?

- ❑ Does every element in the display coordinate together
  in a cohesive manner?

- ❑ Is there an attractive, interesting or attention grabbing
  theme?

- ❑ Are the products and literature elevated?

- ❑ Is lighting used to illuminate the display, graphics or
  products?

- ❑ Do the graphics have the Wow Factor?

- ❑ Is there an interactive game or contest used to obtain
  leads?

By carefully crafting your exhibit's image and appearance even
a small company can look as impressive and influential as a

much larger competitor. Make sure the completed design is consistent with the personality and professionalism promised in your advertising and delivered by your staff. You have succeeded in creating a dynamic display when every element is integrated into a cohesive environment and exemplifies your company image and clearly states the most important benefits to the customer.

A word about booth security

Do not be naive about how safe your products, exhibit and personal items are at a tradeshow. No one wants to assume any exhibitor, attendee or worker at the show would be dishonest, but it is wise to take precautions to prevent any opportunities that might invite theft. It is not that uncommon to hear of plasma screens disappearing off walls, computers gone missing and purses being lost. Take personal responsibility and make a plan to protect your company and employees from any mishaps. Keep small items and valuables hidden inside counters or cabinets while the show is open. Firmly secure expensive products on shelves or in cases so they do not get carried away when you are not looking. At night lock computers, electronics and expensive products away or simply take them with you. Cover tables, counters and shelves of goods with a cloth to hide what is underneath. Keep a close eye on inventory so you can immediately discover any inconsistencies. If the show does not provide security for the exhibits at night and your exhibit is full of expensive items, consider hiring security yourself, just to be sure you are protected.

Pick Your Perfect Structure or Style

Display hardware refers to the physical structure or backdrop that you place in your booth space, as well as all the fixtures you use to merchandise your products. This hardware comes in a variety of forms and styles and is manufactured from many different materials. It might be as simple as a few folding tables under a canvas tent or as elaborate as a professionally made pop-up, panel system, tension fabric display or modular unit. It could also be a unique, one-of-a-kind custom exhibit built with wooden hard walls and laminate panels from your blueprint specifications. Your show marketing budget will dictate whether you work with a professional custom exhibit builder, portable systems distributor or build it yourself.

Portable displays

Portable displays come in a variety of styles, sizes and configurations. There are mini displays that pack up in a briefcase, folding and collapsible units that set on a table, or free-standing floor displays that can stack eight to twelve feet in the air. They can be rented, leased to own or purchased outright. They are lightweight, easy to assemble and designed to set up in minutes without tools. They are designed for easy transport by common carrier, such as UPS or FedEx, taken aboard an airplane or shipped by truck. Considering the expensive fees charged by the convention services companies that control many exhibit halls around the country, portables offer a way to curb the costs associated with shipping, drayage, labor and handling. Many ten or twenty foot portable displays can be wheeled in by a single individual and set up in under 30 minutes. The more elaborate portable and modular displays are manufactured with materials that are lightweight to save on shipping costs, but offer semi-custom features that give them a more substantial appearance.

Portable displays are very economical for the small business owner. Their modular components can be rearranged, interchanged and expanded to accommodate many booth sizes and different uses making them ideal for all types of businesses. Many manufacturers offer both panel and pop-up varieties that include the ability to connect one type with the other for maximum versatility. Portables not only set up in minutes with no tools and cost less than custom displays, they also weigh much less. This helps reduce shipping costs to and from the show and saves money on installation and dismantling services at the event. Below are some of the styles and features of some of the most popular portable displays on the market today.

Panel systems

Panel systems, sometimes referred to as modular displays, are very sturdy. Some panels are constructed of a hard corrugated interior substrate, while others use a plastic or metal frame. Either style can be covered by non-removable, Velcro compatible fabric, permanent or removable graphics or with a variety of colorful laminate or fabric skins. The panels are either accordion hinged tops, middles and bottoms that stack one on top of the other, or individual panels that interconnect with pins or metal splines. They can have either an exterior or interior framing system. Panel systems can be one-sided or reversible so both sides provide display area. They come in tabletop or floor models. One of the panel system's outstanding features is their ability to be used in a variety of configurations. Not only can they stand freely as a floor display, but many can also break into tabletop units or configure as a tower.

Pop-up displays

Pop-up displays are brilliantly engineered and feature a unique, light- weight aluminum, fiberglass or plastic telescoping frame. They start out in compact form for easy packing, and then telescope out into a framework of interlocking bars, struts and pivots, much like an umbrella. Thin Velcro-compatible fabric or photographic mural panels magnetically attach to the framework with metal or plastic channel bars. Pop-up displays offer a smooth, seamless look for graphics applications. They come in flat or arc styles with curved or angular ends. Although they can be double-sided, they cannot reconfigure like panel systems. Tabletop and floor models are available from most manufacturers.

Fabric exhibits

If ease of setup, flexible configurations and lightweight shipping are your requirements, then tension fabric exhibits are the perfect choice for you. Many manufacturers have combined the simplicity of the popup frame and added spandex fabric printed with brilliantly colored inks that fold down with the frame and expand out when opened for a gorgeous, wrinkle-free mural of artwork. Some brands offer geometric structures that use plastic, metal or fiberglass bendable rods and massive sails of colorful fabric imprinted or not, to form triangles, domes, circles and other shapes that can soar thirty feet or more in the air. These can be used to create the entire exhibit or combine to compliment both portable and custom display creations.

A new contemporary style exhibit structure uses aluminum extruded metal posts as a foundation to support tension fabric graphics. Laminate panels are used to enhance the walls of the display and for constructing cabinets, counters and shelves to expand the environment.

Banner stands

One of the most popular display products on the market today is the versatile banner stand. There are many different varieties to choose from. There are tension pole styles that hold vinyl or fabric graphics; telescoping poles that support graphics clipped to the top and bottom support bars or from dowels slipped through a rod pocket in the artwork; and there are posts that support artwork that can be cut to the shape of a person or the products. The most popular units are the retractable types. The graphic is printed on vinyl, paper, fabric or a polycarbonate material. The top or bottom of the artwork has an extension of material that is wound onto a roller in the canister that sets on the floor or hangs on top of a display. The graphic pulls out from a canister like an old style window shade and is supported upright by a pole from behind. This device can hold one graphic on the front and one on the back. They can pull out from the base in thirds and work on a table or a floor. They also come with removable graphic cartridges for an easy exchange of images. They average units are 30" to 68" in width and 78" to 92" in height and can be placed side by side to form a solid wall of graphic art. One brand offers a retractable fabric panel that allows for other graphics to be easily attached and interchanged.

Accessories

Many types of merchandising accessories are available for most brands of displays. Bracket standards, grid or slat wall panels allow the use of fixtures such as shelves, baskets, waterfall racks, hooks, bins and literature holders that can be used to showcase clothing, containers, products and brochures. Recessed shelving units, shelves suspended by wires or cutouts in a display provide placement for video monitors that mount on a stand behind the exhibit. They can be used with a light bar to back light a color transparency or illuminate products or services. Many types of counters are available that stand by themselves or attach to the display. Some companies offer convenient conversion kits that turn shipping cases into podiums thereby eliminating the need to store the cases. Heavy metal truss can be used to support large lighting fixtures or electronics. Folding truss, which is easy to assemble, is a popular accessory in both custom and portable exhibit designs.

Custom displays

The sky is the limit when it comes to building custom exhibits. You are only restricted by your company's budget and the designer's imagination. A firm specializing in custom displays can start with an idea out of your head, design the display, draw the blueprints and present a computer generated, three-dimensional rendering that will bring your creation to life. It can be a small inline exhibit or an enormous two-story structure. You can select from numerous construction materials such as wood, metal, pressed board and laminates. Then, they will build it, crate it, send it to the show, set it up, take it down, ship it back to your office or store it for you. Custom displays are expensive to build and costly to ship, install and dismantle, but the impression you make with a unique, one-of-a-kind display will give you a distinctive look that will set you apart from the crowd.

Buying a display off the internet

On any given day you can find hundreds of tradeshow exhibits, both new and used, advertised on the Internet. There are entire sites dedicated to selling used products. E-Bay and other auction sites are full of options for anyone looking for a bargain.

If you have no brand preference or concerns about customer service, quality and warranties, then you might want to purchase an exhibit off the Internet. Just remember that you get what you pay for. The guy who stockpiles hardware in his garage and offers it to you from an on-line store, probably cannot deliver the repair you might need when a part breaks while you're setting up in another state. The online purchase most likely does not include a professional consultation with your sales staff on how to conceptualize your marketing message and transfer that to the graphic mural that will draw customers to your booth. If you are serious about your professional image and want your display investment to return profits to you for years to come, it would be advisable to work with a reputable exhibit company, selling quality brands, with staff on board that will look out for your best interests and be there to assure your best results. If you just cannot pass up that really cheap Internet deal, then at least take it to a local display company that will help you complete your tradeshow presence and become your resource for success.

Make it yourself

Many small, non-profit and start-up companies have limited funds with which to develop a display. Lots of creativity, imagination and resourcefulness, however, can make up for lack of money. In addition, there are artists and crafters that require more rustic or hand made styles of product displays for their art shows and street fairs. The following low- cost construction materials and items can be used to create an attractive and effective display to showcase your merchandise and services until you can afford to purchase a professionally constructed display. If you do decide to make your own display, remember that the customer forms an opinion of your professionalism, performance and quality of product or service by what they initially see at your booth.

Shelves

Shelves offer versatility in the display area, but they must be easy to transport and simple to assemble to be practical. One of the most popular ways to make shelves for a portable display is to use a wooden, three-panel screen as a base and use 1' x 6' plywood boards as shelves. Another shelf display can be made by attractively painting two, 6' stepladders and placing plywood boards or wooden dowels across each rung of the ladder. There also are commercial shelves available at store fixture companies.

Panels

Panels form the basis of many interesting and effective displays. Many are lightweight and easy for one person to handle. Panels are versatile and can be used in a variety of configurations. In addition, many low-cost materials such as pegboard, lattice, metal grids and grooved wallboard can be used to construct display panels.

Framed artwork, calligraphy or photography needs a backdrop to be effectively displayed. Pegboard is an excellent display material, since it is very versatile and inexpensive. An "X" frame or "A" frame display can be fashioned from pegboard. These display styles are easy to erect and transport. Another option is to construct a triangular display of pegboard. This style allows three sides for displaying products.

Pegboards

If you place hooks or piping around the perimeter of an exhibit area, 4' x 6' sheets of pegboard can be hung to provide a flat display surface. Another alternative is to mount sheets of pegboard on wooden or metal legs. A variety of metal hooks, Plexiglas display pieces and shelf fixtures are made specifically for use with pegboard. You can find these items at outlets that sell store display fixtures.

Wire grid panels

Wire grid panels can be assembled in a variety of ways, and can easily be expanded to fit your changing needs. Many accessories and display attachments such as baskets, shelves, hooks, railings and trays can be purchased for use with wire grids. Wire grids can create a very professional, contemporary display that is durable too. They are, however, expensive and very heavy to transport and erect.

Lattice

An inexpensive, but attractive material to use in a display is wooden lattice. Found at most building supply stores, lattice is usually available in 4' x 8' sheets. Don't buy flimsy lattice primarily used for garden plants and flowers. Use lattice with thick diagonal slats. This material is excellent for displaying items that should be hung, such as clothing or dried flower arrangements. Hang lattice in the same manner as pegboard, from piping around the perimeter of the booth. Lattice panels also can be mounted on legs or made into folding screens.

Modular wire cubes

Modular cubes are popular and are an inexpensive alternative to heavy, metal wire grids. Small and easy to assemble, the cubes are made of lightweight, plastic-coated wire panels that snap together with plastic connectors. Assemble an entire wall of cubes or a small custom unit to display shirts, gift items, sporting goods or any stackable merchandise. Mini grids come in several colors and utilize the same accessories as heavy wire grids.

Slat wall panels

Slat wall panels, also known as grooved wallboard, are a multi-purpose display material. Heavy grooved slat wall comes in 4' x 8' sheets, which can be cut, to any size. The grooves separating each slat of wood are designed to hold display fixtures such as hooks, baskets, and shelves. The panels come ready to paint, laminated in colored finishes or finished in a variety of wood veneers.

Get organized

Start getting organized by making lists of all the products and materials you will take with you to an event. Create a list for each category of items. Such categories would include sales tools, literature, cashiering supplies, purchase orders, display items, personal necessities and product inventory. Post a list of all items to be packed on the outside of the container they are stored in so the staff knows where everything is when it arrives. Check off each item as you pack it for shipping or load it into your car. This may seem like a time consuming idea, but

...ciate the logic the first time you forget the cable ...omputer, your cash box, keys to your monitor case or ... container of company brochures. Look over the list below to see what applies to your business.

SALES SUPPLIES
- ☐ Lead forms
- ☐ Order forms
- ☐ Business cards
- ☐ Purchase orders
- ☐ Contracts
- ☐ Petty cash
- ☐ Press kit
- ☐ Pens & pencils
- ☐ Calendar
- ☐ Appointment book
- ☐ Envelopes
- ☐ Calculator
- ☐ Receipt book
- ☐ Charge card slips & imprinter
- ☐ Tax chart
- ☐ Sales literature
- ☐ Brochures
- ☐ Product portfolio
- ☐ Samples
- ☐ Cell phone charger

IMPORTANT DOCUMENTS
- ☐ Travel tickets
- ☐ Credit Cards
- ☐ Expense Reports
- ☐ Hotel & car rental confirmations
- ☐ Exhibitor kit
- ☐ Bill of lading
- ☐ Confirmation of advance purchases
- ☐ Staff schedules

TOOLBOX
- ☐ Scissors
- ☐ Velcro
- ☐ Scotch tape & duct tape
- ☐ Rubber bands
- ☐ Stapler, staples & remover
- ☐ Tacks
- ☐ Glue
- ☐ Wire
- ☐ Flashlight
- ☐ String
- ☐ Hammer

DISPLAY ITEMS
- ☐ Display hardware
- ☐ Set-up tools
- ☐ Give-aways
- ☐ Graphics
- ☐ Literature holders
- ☐ Accessories
- ☐ Lights

PERSONAL ITEMS
- ☐ Drinking water & cups
- ☐ Wet towelettes
- ☐ Cough drops
- ☐ Tweezers
- ☐ Nail file
- ☐ Tissues
- ☐ Mouthwash and mints
- ☐ Chapstick
- ☐ Band-Aids
- ☐ Aspirin

Get the most from your investment

Some major corporations exhibit in as many as twenty to fifty events a year. The majority of small businesses exhibit in less than ten shows a year. That leaves a lot of time when the company's display is not being used. Instead of packing up your display after each show and sending it into storage, consider using it for other purposes or in other venues such as those listed here. This way you will be able to amortize the cost and make the display work harder for you.

- Seminars
- Recruiting
- Sponsorship activities
- Sales meetings
- Fund-raisers
- Office communications
- Media events
- Mall marketing
- Reseller support

- Training classes
- Lobby displays
- Information centers
- Special events
- Career days
- Press conferences
- Product displays
- Charity functions
- Employee recognition

TOP TEN TIPS FOR A TERRIFIC DISPLAY

1 Select a display structure that best serves your exhibiting goals and sales people.

2 Plan a creative theme that reinforces your marketing message.

3 Invest in large, dynamic graphics and signs.

4 Create vignettes that showcase what you sell.

5 Incorporate props to enhance product presentation.

6 Use creative methods to elevate products and literature.

7 Dress up the staff to reinforce the theme.

8 Add lighting to draw attention.

9 Color coordinate every element of the display.

10 Make sure the display exemplifies your company image.

Drive Traffic to Your Booth

After your display is complete, it's time to develop clever promotions and advertising methods that will increase traffic, improve sales and provide your company with a competitive edge. Your show success depends on capturing the attention of as many qualified attendees as possible. The smartest exhibitors do not leave this to chance and understand it is not the sole responsibility of the promoter to get customers to your booth. Getting the right customer to your exhibit should be a three-step process that includes promotions before, during and after the show.

Promotions before the show

Start your promotional campaign in advance by soliciting prospects with an incentive that is mailed, faxed, or phoned to them weeks before the show begins. Pre-show promotions are designed to encourage a particular, pre-selected group of people to come to your booth.

A pre-show solicitation can increase traffic to your booth by thirty percent. You can boost that success rate even more if you include a promotional item in your mailing. Your first consideration should be to reach hot prospects, such as those who have inquired about your company recently. Next would be to contact people from your database that visited your booth last year, but have not yet been closed. Any pre-registered attendees, whose names can be obtained from show management, are prime candidates. Your top 50 to 100 best customers would also be another important list to contact.

Pre-show promotions, like all your promotional efforts, should tie into and capitalize on a predetermined marketing theme. Be sure to include your booth number on all materials. For best results, use a series of two or three solicitations before show time. The following examples offer proven, effective ways to solicit a response from prospects.

Make it personal

Send each client a formal invitation to the show along with a complimentary pass to the exhibit hall. Surveys have shown this to be the most effective way to gain the interest of the prospect. Include a map of the host city along with a map of the show site. Draw arrows directing them from the parking lot, through the maze of booths, to your exhibit space on the show floor. Mail a certificate that can be redeemed at your display for a free gift, or a coupon they can exchange for tickets to a reception, seminar or demonstration. If the budget allows, consider a technique called the companion mailer. This two-step idea requires a gift to be sent with your first solicitation accompanied by the promise of a companion gift for visiting the booth. Send a drink coaster with your message printed on it along with the promise of a coffee mug for coming to your booth. Send a ball cap and an offer of a free monogram for visiting your display. Bring the recipe card to the booth and get a complimentary cookbook. Mail them an empty CD jacket with promise of some smooth jazz if they stop by. The ideas are endless if the budget allows. Just make sure it is not a random offering, but one that ties into all the other marketing messages you have incorporated into your sales efforts.

Your second most effective method for pre-show solicitation is email or the fax. Keep it unique and personalized to the target audience. Offer everyone on your list some type of useful information. Send a checklist or matrix comparing your products, benefits and prices to those of the competitors that will be at the show. Provide your industry's "Top Ten Tips" that would benefit their businesses. Offer reprints of any newspaper or magazine articles that offer current research or information that supports your industry or product. A phone call will also boost attendance to your booth. Place a call to the top executives of the largest companies you do business with and personally invite them to the show. Have your sales staff contact their top clients and tie the invitation in with one of the give-aways already discussed. The personal touch always makes a good impression.

Send it and they will come

Sending out an invitation to participate in an enticing game or contest at the booth will increase visitor traffic. Trade show attendees love to play games at the show and they offer great appeal as a pre-show incentive. Some ideas include sending a puzzle piece that they must bring to your booth. If their piece fits into the empty spots on the puzzle displayed at your booth, they win a prize. Mail out a key that could unlock a safe full of prizes, the ignition of a new car, or a treasure chest of cash. One exhibitor, at a tradeshow in Las Vegas, se keys that could unlock an acrylic box filled with $500 gaming chips. Use a scratch ticket with special numbers to be matched at your booth or a bingo card to be used in a game played at the show. One large computer software company sends out DVD's that the customer must insert into a computer at the booth to win prizes. A bank sends out credit cards that must be swiped through a terminal for prizes. Whatever idea you use, make sure it ties into your company's product and the theme of your exhibit. Consult with your display designer about creating a fun pre-show promotion with a clever twist.

PROMOTIONS AT THE SHOW

Hold a demonstration

The Center for Exhibition Industry Research claims that demonstrations are the number one way to create excitement at a trade show and they score the highest in the memory ratings from show attendees. If you aren't sure about demonstrating your product, ask yourself this question. Are you able to manufacture your product right at the booth? I was attending a vendor fair sponsored by a large warehouse chain. In the exhibit hall a broom company was actually making their signature brooms right in front of me. An employee would toss a wooden handle and a measured amount of straw into a large square machine. After a mildly noisy moment, out came a broom on the other side. They handed me the broom as a gift complete with the company's contact information stamped into the handle.

If you can find a way to demonstrate how your product works you will have the makings of a great promotion. Demonstrations have been popularized for years at home shows where many of us have been mesmerized by the slicing and dicing food processors, the commodes that can flush down ten golf balls at once and knives that can cut through a nail. At a builder's expo I took a sledgehammer and failed at my attempt to smash through the protective film covering a sheet of window glass. The crowd that formed around me was very impressed.

Can you show what it's made of? Open it up in layers, display the ingredients or uncover hidden parts. If you've ever attended an auto show you cannot help being drawn over to the car that is completely cut in half exposing a cross section of upholstery, metal and engine parts. I created a way for a telecommunications company to show the insides of their underground cable. We stripped 8" of casing off the cable bundle exposing its colorful grouping of wires inside. We then bent the wires to look like a floral bouquet, placed the 4"-thick arrangement into a beautiful vase and created an eye-catching prop for all to touch and feel.

What can a service business, that has no tangible product, demonstrate? An insurance company can calculate retirement projections and a health care facility can offer cholesterol screenings. A financial planner used a marketing theme that told visitors to take the stress out of investing. He offered free foot massages at his booth.

If your product doesn't lend itself to an on-site demonstration, then use technology to assist you. A 90-second repeating loop video, computer software program, slide show, artist's story board, photo portfolio or multi-media presentation can provide customers with information that may stimulate them to buy. Show your product in use by your customers. Take the customer on a buying trip, tour them through your store or follow your staff through the manufacturing plant. Demonstrate how your products are transported to the stores or reveal where the raw materials come from. Customers crave inside secrets and information not readily revealed to the public. Did you grow up watching *Mr. Roger's Neighborhood?* Remember how interesting and informative the trips to the crayon and potato chip factories were? Current shows like *How It's Made* and *Made in America* confirm our desire for interesting details about how things come to be on the shelves of the stores we shop at. If you can use a demonstration that is relevant to your product or service you will capture the audience's attention, improve the customer's knowledge and leave a lasting impression about your business.

Give a live presentation

Every year companies seek out new ways to draw customers and out-promote the competition. Elaborate sales presentations are cleverly disguised as entertainment by using lavish musical reviews, comedy acts, dancers, game shows, multimedia presentations, virtual reality, Hollywood style productions, pool sharks, fortune tellers and magicians. Some companies employ professional models, actors or special trade show production companies to create personalized presentations, while others use employees to accomplish the task. Live presentations can capture large audiences, but they must be carefully choreographed so the objective of qualifying prospects and capturing valuable market information is accomplished.

Put your customers to work

One of the most well received techniques for increasing traffic is to staff your booth with satisfied customers. Prospects love to know what your customers think about you. They feel more comfortable talking to real people who love your product than to salespeople with an agenda. Your greatest salesperson is your best customer. Invite them to join you for a specified time each day. Brief them on their duties then let them speak to visitors at the booth. Bring attention to your star by providing special attire or give them a name badge that distinguishes them from the rest of the staff. Be sure to promote this networking opportunity in your pre-show solicitations and advertising. Reward your customer guest for their assistance and time with some of your products, tickets to a show, dinner or a special gift.

Feature a personality

If you really want to draw a crowd, secure the appearance of a local sports figure, media celebrity or politician. You can hire "The Hulk" for $3500 or "The Beav" for $5000, but if you want a celebrity like Emeril to cook up a promotion for you be prepared to pay $100,000. If that's too expensive just hire a celebrity look-a-like or rent a robot. These special guests can sign autographs, demonstrate your product, hand out samples or pass around your literature. You don't even need a live person. If you're on a tight budget, you need only to purchase a life-size cardboard photographic replica of a famous person or sports star and let customers pose for pictures with them. Attendees love this type of promotion and will bring friends back to experience it. Just remember to keep the promotion in tune with your theme.

Play a game

Interactive games are very popular. They draw attention and help the staff open dialog with prospective clients. Make the game fun and integrate it into the company theme and marketing strategy. People love to spin a wheel, pick a card, throw a ball, press a button or turn a dial to win a prize. My company created a successful contest for a phone company that sold pay phones. We built a replica of a pay phone out of clear acrylic complete with push buttons and a clear receiver with all the electrical workings visible. The phone company even provided the authentic coin stickers and instructions for the prop so it looked exactly like a real working pay phone. We filled it with money and held a contest to guess how much was inside. A sign on the top read "guess how much money you're missing without a pay phone at your business." The amount inside corresponded to an estimate of profit from one year of pay phone calls. The attendee would leave a business card with their guess on the back and receive a small change purse as a thank you gift. The winner of the game got a real working replica of a pay phone for their home. The customers were easily attracted to the unusual prop and had fun playing the game. The sales people loved the game because they had a great conversation starter that lead right into a product discussion. Use your imagination to develop an interactive game that will help promote your message, attract your clientele and generate leads and sales.

Offer samples

Your products will be much more intriguing to the visitor when they are able to touch, feel, smell or taste them. How many times have you returned to a booth with the samples of dip and bean soup and ended up buying the show special of buy three get one free? Anytime the prospect can interact with and experience your product you have an advantage. People will always stop at the booth that offers samples to eat or drink but food is not the only thing you can successfully sample. An interior design firm might give away pieces of carpet or fabric swatches. A stationery company could give out samples of textured or colored paper. One copier company provides color copies of any photo the customer has in their wallet. A clever powder coating company cut pipes

that were powder coated in a variety of colors into one inch
pieces and placed the colorful samples in a basket for anyone
to take along. Service businesses can sample things like eye
exams, insurance cost comparisons, foot massages or jewelry
cleaning.

I want to mention an irritating phenomenon that is sweeping
tradeshows and consumer shows everywhere. There seems to
be an unusually large number of exhibitors that place bowls or
baskets of candy at their booth. What is the purpose of this?
It's not Halloween. Does it qualify prospects? Does it
encourage interaction with your sales staff? I don't think so.
There is no benefit to feeding the attendees calorie-laden
sweets. Most of the time people simply grab a handful of
kisses as they fly by your space. Unless you actually sell the
candy or treats given away or the offerings tie into your
overall environment save your money.

Hold a drawing

Nearly every exhibit you pass has some sort of drawing to
entice you in. Drawings offer an easy way to obtain the
prospects' personal information for follow-up after the show.
When you use a drawing to attract attention, it helps to
increase response if you display the prize. Make sure it is
something associated with your product or service. Give away
an item that requires installation or additional parts or service
so you can connect with them again at a later date. Where
possible, require the winner to pick up the prize at your store
or warehouse or make them go to your website to redeem it.
Exhibit Experts gives away one free tabletop display rental
valued at $350. The winners are delighted and come to the
showroom to look at their options and book their rental
date. A consultant discusses accessories and graphics that
would enhance their prize, which usually results in an

additional sale and a new customer. If you want to encourage attendees to return to your booth numerous times throughout the show then select multiple winners each day and post their names on a winners board at periodic intervals for everyone to view.

Make it easy to participate in the drawing by providing lead slips to fill out that request their name, address and phone number or a place for them to drop their business card. Be sure to ask a few qualifying questions from each entrant and make notes on the back of their lead slip or business card as to what their needs are so follow-up will be easier.

Furnish give-aways

Trade show attendees have come to expect interesting freebies from the exhibits they visit and will seek out the best selections. Everyone loves to receive them and a creative, useful give-away could make your company the hit of the show. Don't waste your money on any random item. To give your freebie maximum impact, make sure it reinforces your marketing efforts so the message goes home with them along with the trinket. Get creative. Here are a few ideas to illustrate the point. A plumber hands out plungers with the company information stamped into the handle. A pest control business gives away fly swatters when a guest fills out a lead card. A swimming pool manufacturer hands out sun block, visors and beach balls. A computer software company rewards visitors to the booth with screen savers or monitor brushes.

Exhibitors often make the common mistake of leaving their give-aways out on the table for anyone to grab. Have you ever attendee stop by your booth just to shove a handful of pens into their bag? It's pretty frustrating, but it all the time. To protect yourself from this bad habit, only a few of the promotional products at the booth.

87

Store the rest out of sight. Make prospects work for their free gift. Don't just stand at the counter and hand them over to anyone who passes by. Get their business card, have them fill out a survey card or sit and watch the demonstration in order to receive the gift. When you have a game or contest at your booth to draw traffic use the freebie as a reward for playing. Mail a premium along with your offer in a pre-show mailing.

The success of your promotional item or premium give-away is only restricted by your creativity and budget. While we are on the subject of budget, how do you calculate how many give-a-way items to bring to the show? Never bring as many as you think you should because the staff will surely hand them out at random just so they don't have to ship them back to the office after the show closes. Consider that only about 16 percent of attendees at the show will be qualified to buy from you and only 3 percent of those will even be interested. A simple rule of thumb, if you are really looking to use them to engage prospects or reward customers, is to bring one hundred for every one thousand attendees or about 10 percent.

Teach a seminar

Many consumer shows, tradeshows and conventions offer educational seminars to the attendees during the event. If you have good presentation skills and possess valuable information to share or a talent to teach, then you could be eligible to become a speaker and conduct an industry-related workshop, seminar or panel discussion for attendees or the public at large. This type of opportunity provides a great selling advantage. As a seminar presenter you will be able to focus on your products in detail and profile your company to a captive audience. Such an opportunity will elevate your credibility and showcase yourself as an expert. It will increase your ability to promote your business, as you will be able to promote your seminar at the booth and promote your booth at the seminar. Another advantage to giving a seminar is that you will receive additional, free recognition and advertising in the show program that is handed out to all the attendees.

Use bag stuffers

Here is a simple way to get free advertising and set your business apart from the crowd. Ask show management for permission to place a promotional solicitation inside the free exhibitor packets that are given out in bags at the entry into the show. Put your brochure, an advertising premium or an invitation to visit your booth into the bag. I recently suggested this idea to a client who was going to attend a large industry conference and expo. Out of the entire list of exhibitors, their company was the only one that had literature in the bag. This did not go unnoticed by the competitors who wanted to know why my client received special treatment. My client was pleased to explain to everyone that all they had to do was ask for this favor and it was granted. No one else had thought of that.

Donate a door prize

Inquire as to whether the promoter of the event is giving away door prizes or holding an auction during the show. Different from the drawings by individual exhibitors, these event-sponsored promotions create excitement for all attendees throughout the entire length of the show. You may find the request for a door prize donation in the Exhibitor Kit you receive weeks prior to the show. The promoter will often display the donated gifts in the lobby, or at the very least, promote the prize and the donor's identity free of charge in the event program. Sometimes the winners of the prizes and the donating companies will be announced over the intercom so everyone on the show floor can hear the news. If an auction is featured, then your donation will be center stage with a description of the gift and your company information next to it at the auction table for all to see. That's terrific advertising for only the cost of the prize you donate.

Be a sponsor

Get an extra boost of exposure by taking advantage of the many sponsorship options provided by the organization producing the event. Some options include donating the attendee bags, hosting a bar or food station, providing lanyards, name tags, flowers for the lunch tables, directional signage or lunch table gifts. Being a sponsor is a great way to show support for the organization and receive prominent positioning in the process.

Use door hangers

When the trade show draws out of town exhibitors the hotels usually have blocks of rooms or entire floors devoted to the attendees. Send a staff member to place a door hanger advertisement on the door knob or slide a promotional flyer under each hotel room door. This way your advertising won't get lost among the hundreds of solicitations they will receive at the show. Some hotels even offer this as a service to your business. Check to make sure the hotel has no policy prohibiting this.

Hospitality suites

Many companies will book a separate hotel or conference room in addition to, or sometimes in place of, a booth space. This room is located away from the show floor and can serve many purposes. It can be used to entertain clients, serve as a private conference room for more elaborate sales efforts or for showcasing products in more detail. Invitations can be sent to special clients in advance or attendees can be pre-screened at the show and invited there. Hospitality suites are always well received by customers and are very effective tools for promotion.

Program ads

Consider designating a small amount of your budget to advertising in publications directed at attendees of specific shows. You will get the best results from trade journals and magazines that promote the show. Another option is to purchase an ad in the show program. The rates are usually very reasonable and the program has an extended shelf life. Be sure to mention your booth number in the ad and offer an incentive for stopping by.

Collateral and business cards

It's amazing how many times I've walked the show floor on the last day of the event to find that many exhibitors have run out of brochures and business cards. Never run out of business cards at the booth and always carry an adequate supply wherever you go. It is important to be prepared with enough sales tools to get you through the entire event. To conserve costs, customize an inexpensive sales flyer for mass distribution. Provide an enticing show special on one side of the flyer and include a call to action along with a deadline date. On the reverse side offer features about your company and how you stand out from the competition, along with the most important benefits a customer will receive when they

⁺ to do business with you. You can give these away to one but, save your expensive, four color brochures for qualified buyers. Keep them under the counter and only offer them to those attendees who ask for them or to those who show true interest in your offerings. It is not uncommon to see salespeople positioned at the entrance to their exhibit randomly handing out expensive information packets without any effort to qualify or even ask any questions of the attendee. Your product literature is not a substitute for selling, just a sales support device. Consider what you do when you return to the hotel room with bags of brochures you've collected from the show. You toss the majority of them into the trash.

Sales Strategies for the Tradeshow Environment

Attitude is everything

I am sure you have heard the selling motto that states people buy from people they like. This is such a truism, because no matter how wonderful your products are, how great your exhibit looks or how skilled your sales team is, none of that matters if customers don't like you. If you appear unfriendly or indifferent they will pass right by. If you look preoccupied or unprofessional they won't stop. Unfortunately, they may not stop if they don't like your body language, appearance or the clothes you are wearing. A professional image, good grooming, acting friendly and attentive are all areas everyone has control of and can achieve improvement in. Of all the elements that create the customers first impression of you, attitude is the most important. If you are new to sales you may be apprehensive about the selling process. Maybe you have a fear of rejection, don't want to seem too pushy or are not sure what to say. With the help of the following sales strategy you will be able to find that sales personality that will make you friendly, but not too aggressive, informative, but not too pushy and enthusiastic, but not overbearing. Study and use the skills outlined here and you will feel confident that when you step into that exhibit booth as a representative of your company you will exude enthusiasm, project confidence and possess an inviting manner in both your actions and words.

Selecting your booth staff

How do you select the people that will represent your company at the show? What criteria do you use to make the best choices? Do you recruit the most experienced sales people or those with the best personalities? Do you include a mix of technical and engineering experts on your team? Do you send those people not likely to be missed at the office? Maybe you just ask for volunteers, pick the team at random or simply draft people, at the last minute, who would really rather not go.

You will be making a significant investment in every show you exhibit, so here is a word to the wise. Your return on investment is directly tied to the quality and dependability of the employees you send to the show. Horrors abound that will make you think twice about your choices. Management is usually the last to know about the unbelievable mishaps and embarrassing behaviors that occur on the road. Let me give you a few examples that are all too common. These are all true stories that my staff or I have personally witnessed.

- The team leader misses her appointment to meet the installation supervisor to confirm which booth configuration she wants to use because she could not wait to go shopping at the boutique across the street. To avoid letting four laborers stand around doing nothing at $75 per hour, the crew sets up the booth the way they think it should go. When she arrives 30 minutes before the show opens and discovers the booth is set up completely wrong there is no time to make changes.

- Your top two salesmen stroll in 30 minutes after the show opens and they are still drunk from a night of partying. They openly joke about their hangovers throughout the day. They don't notice the strong smell of alcohol they are emitting, but the customers do.

- Your staff was in a hurry to take down the booth so they could go play golf. Someone left the bill of lading on the counter and it never got filed at the service desk. The freight gets forced and you get a bill for an extra $3000.

- You just spent a fortune on brand-new, four color corporate brochures to hand out at the show. You send five full boxes to the booth. Attendance was underestimated and there are four boxes left when the show closes. Your sales person is too lazy to prepare them to ship back so she dumps them in the garbage.

Preparing your sales team

One of the most startling revelations I've discovered in my tradeshow travels is the fact that so few companies train their exhibit staff how to sell and represent the company at the show. There are thousands of dollars spent on booth space, elaborate exhibits and graphics to brand the company. Hundreds more are spent to take the top sales staff out of the office, fly them to the show, put them up in the best hotels and feed them while they are there. Then they are turned loose to sell at the booth with no training. No tradeshow sales training, that is. Does this sound like your company?

The fact is that show attendees are tired of dealing with untrained exhibit personnel that appear unprepared, preoccupied or don't have the right answers to their questions about your products and services. Management might be dissatisfied with the closing ratio or number of leads generated. Part of the problem regarding training your booth staff lies in the fact that sales people are inherently ego driven and may not welcome changes to their selling procedures. Don't let the seasoned sales people bully management into omitting this procedure.

It is very important to select your booth staff with care. Statistics from the Center for Exhibition Industry Research claim that 85 percent of tradeshow attendees base their opinion of your company on the actions of your employees at the booth. This is why it is essential to train and prepare them with a game plan before you even think about letting them step inside your booth. It is a good idea to hold a meeting before the show to discuss responsibilities and duties. Set clear goals, outline your expectations and make them accountable for their actions and behavior. Clarify everything before hand so time and money are not wasted.

You can teach old dogs new tricks if you dangle the right bones. Need more convincing? See if you recognize similarities to anyone on your staff in the following example. Each sales person uses their own special presentation to engage prospects. Every presentation is different so there is no congruent message being relayed to the prospective customers. The staff sits down often and has long conversation with one another or with exhibitors in the neighboring booths. They pass out expensive brochures to everyone who comes by without qualification. When the show is over they're left with few leads and no sales to take back to management. They can't understand why the results are so poor. What do they do? They complain and make excuses! They blame poor productivity on the traffic or booth location. They tell you, "Nobody was qualified," or "the promoter didn't spend enough on advertising." The real problem with your staff is that they were not given any sales strategy or incentive to perform. They had no goal requirements and were not offered a plan of action. Seven out of ten companies put staff in the booth with no exhibitor training because they assume sales skills from the field translate onto the show floor. Unfortunately, poor results from a show are often due to this misconception.

Selling at a trade show is not like a regular sales call. You cannot sell the same way you do in the field. In the fast-paced environment of the trade and consumer show arena the rules of engagement are different from the selling that takes place in your office, your store, on an outside sales call or on the telephone. For one thing, the atmosphere at an event is noisy and full of distractions. There is enormous competition for attention, not much time to make your point and no way to really prepare in advance for the many different customer inquiries. Instead of having 45 minutes to make a presentation to a captive audience, a sales person has only a short time to translate a message to a customer who will be walking past your space in a matter of seconds.

A random sales approach is not effective here. You must establish optional qualifying questions to draw them over. Develop four or five statements to excite and educate them about your benefits and features. Make sure each customer is receiving the same information from each representative. Be certain to obtain contact information for future follow-up. If you want to close more sales and increase the number of qualified leads your booth staff collects, then script a formal, written sales presentation designed exclusively for the show and require each team member to memorize it an use it consistently.

Maybe you believe your staff doesn't need training because

they know how to sell or have been on your sales force for years. That does not matter in this case. The problem is that without a consistent presentation from each person or accountability from the entire team, management will never be able to calculate a return on investment. There will be no way to discover why one salesperson gets fifty leads and another gets ten. It is known that at any given show only 16 percent of the attendees will be interested in your product. Of those, an even smaller percentage will be qualified to buy. If you want to guarantee that their time is spent wisely and your investment is protected, you must train your staff.

Before the show hold a staff meeting and review the goals, presentations, expectations and incentive programs to be implemented for the event. Preparing your staff ensures your best impression. It's important to look better, act better and sell better than the competition, because attendees will be comparing you to them in the next aisle. The staff's knowledge of your products and services, as well as their enthusiasm and attentiveness to the customers are important to your plan, but it's the carefully prepared sales strategy that determines your success.

After the show closes hold a debriefing meeting at the show location or schedule it for back at the office when everyone returns. Discuss what went right and what went wrong throughout the show. Have the staff critique each others performance and offer suggestions for improvement. Evaluate the benefits of the show, discuss whether the goals were achieved, determine if the show was valuable and assign follow up duties. The results received from this final step should be the determining factor as to whether you return to that show again next year or drop it from your event schedule.

Your formula for selling success

Exhibitor selling requires "Persuasive Conversation." You must remember that your biggest competitor is time. You have only about seven seconds to make contact and less than a minute to deliver your message and qualify the prospect. Therefore, before you can get a lead, book an appointment or make a sale, you must first influence the customer to stop long enough to talk to you. Think of it this way: your number one goal at a trade show is not to persuade a customer to buy, but to persuade them to listen. How exactly do you put this good advice to work? Closing a sale at a consumer show requires even more refined selling skills. The following step-by-step instructions will help you develop your own game plan, thereby increasing your profits and maximizing your chances for selling success.

Whether you are retailing products and taking payments at a consumer show or giving information and generating leads at a tradeshow, the selling formula is much the same. You must grab their attention, qualify their interest, and explain what you do, how it will help them and why they need it. The next step is to close the sale or get the contact information to follow-up with later. The presentation does not have to be complicated, just effective, efficient and consistent. To make it very easy for anyone to sell a product, service or an idea at a show the following simple formula can be used.

The Five E's of exhibitor selling –
Engage, Excite, Educate, Encourage and Exit

Your first step to success must be to ENGAGE the prospect in conversation. Then proceed to EXCITE them about all the benefits they will receive and EDUCATE them as to how your product or service will deliver those things. Then depending on how they have responded to your qualifying questions you will ENCOURAGE them to do something, such as make a purchase, give you a lead or set up an appointment. If they aren't qualified, you will disengage yourself and EXIT from the conversation so you can move on to a more qualified prospect. To make your time at any show worthwhile it is critical that each salesperson speak to as many people as possible in order to reach as many targeted prospects as possible. Remember, you only have a few moments to find them, qualify them, close them and dismiss them.

Let's analyze each element of the Five E's sales formula separately.

Engage

Don't just stand there and watch the crowd walk by your booth. Be pro-active and make eye contact with a prospect and direct them over to you. As you glance down the aisle at the people approaching your display, be on the lookout for customer cues. If you have followed the suggestions in this book, your display should capture their interest and make them pause for a closer look. They may be dazzled by your colorful graphics, stop to read your signs, grab a brochure as they walk by, or venture in to look at your merchandise. Look them in the eyes as they approach, motion them over and engage them in conversation using your personal lead lines. Lead lines are pre-arranged questions or statements that compel the prospect to stop and talk to you. Review the samples that follow and select the types of lead lines that best fit your personality and selling style.

The easiest lead line to use is the common denominator. Make a habit of looking at everyone's name badge. Many shows code the badges by color indicating the attendee's status, such as buyer, vendor, exhibitor, or manufacturer. The badge may also provide you with information as to their company name, position or city they live in. If you notice they are from your home town, you could open the conversation by mentioning that you grew up there too and inquire where they went to high school or ask about a local landmark.

What is the attendee wearing? Do they have on T-shirts promoting a sports team or an association logo? Comment on the team's latest performance or ask about their affiliation with that organization. You might say, "Those Phoenix Suns really got the job done last night, didn't they?" Or approach them by saying, "I see your shirt says Kansas City Rotary. Are you a member of the Rotary?"

What are they carrying? Did they pick up a clever give-away from one of the other exhibitors? Ask them where they got it or what booth they like the best. Be friendly. The objective of this approach is to find a common denominator that encourages conversation with the prospect. Once a rapport is established, you can proceed with additional questions to gauge their interest in your wares.

These soft approaches are the easiest and least aggressive ways to open dialog with prospects and work best for beginners. If you are an experienced salesperson with a bolder personality you will want to open the conversation with an interesting statement, statistic or qualifying question like one of these. "You look like you could use our latest foot massager!" "Does your company exhibit in tradeshows?" "How would you like to go on the fishing trip of a lifetime? Step over here and I will show you our award-wining software program." "I bet you've never seen a kitchen faucet like this before." "Did you hear that we just won our Industry's Merit Ribbon for Quality?" "My division sold more than 1,000 of these copiers last month. Does your company have one?" Stay away from boring, insincere openers that give the customer an easy out. Try to avoid openers like, "Can I help you?" or "How are you today?" or " How's the show going so far?" Get creative and craft statements that get the answers you need, fast. If your lead line worked, you now have their attention and know that they are qualified.

Excite

It is now time for you to EXCITE them about your product, service, organization or company. In four or five statements explain how your offerings will benefit them and solve their most difficult problems. If you know your target audience you will know their most important issues. Their most difficult pain. Will your product make them smarter, healthier, safer? Will your service make them wealthier or happier? The main emphasis should be on what's in it for them.

Educate

The next few statements will outline what you do and reinforce how you will give them those benefits. Keep in mind that you must deliver all of this information in just a few minutes. If you've made a good connection, the customer will start asking you technical questions or inquire about the product's performance, quality, availability, price or color. These are buying indicators that show strong customer interest and should serve as your cue to ENCOURAGE them to do something.

Encourage

What is your goal at this point in the process? What do you want the customer to do? If you are at a selling show this would be the time to close the sale. You could have them fill out the lead card, watch the demonstration or participate in your survey. Decide on the specific closing statements beforehand. "I can ship this copier to your office by next Friday, Mr. Smith, if you would like to take advantage of our

10% show discount today." "We have one more spot on this spectacular cruise. Can we get you booked right now?" "Did you want just one of the party dips or the three for five special?" Prepare for a variety of objections beforehand. Brainstorm with your sales people to uncover the most common objections and the effective responses and rebuttals for each. If you can't make the sale immediately, ask for a purchase order and ship the product later. Schedule a sales call at their office to explain the product further. Make arrangements for a demonstration at your facility. Invite them to visit your store or order products later on line.

Sometimes the prospect is on the verge of a commitment, but needs a little push. Provide an incentive to buy from you immediately. Offer a show special with a discounted price. Give free shipping on orders placed at the show. Include extra merchandise with a purchase executed that day. Give a gift with purchase or a two for one offer. Prepackage a grouping of products that make it easy to buy immediately and will encourage multiple sales. If nothing works and you realize you will not get an immediate commitment, then you must EXIT.

Exit

Always remember that prospecting is a numbers game. It's not productive to have long discussions with talkative, unqualified prospects or to spend extra time with someone who is not ready to buy. The longer you spend with one person, the more hot prospects are walking past your booth. If the people you are talking to are good leads, obtain their names and follow-up information then go to the next person. When you discover the person is not a qualified prospect, you must politely dismiss them and move on to someone else. Hand them a brochure and politely say, "Thanks for stopping by Ms. Jones. Please review our brochure and call us when you have a need for our services." Or you could say, "It was nice meeting you, please keep our brochure for future reference." Shake their hand, smile, and turn in the other direction to make eye contact with the next prospect.

Never lose site of your goals and the purpose for being at the show. You will never be able to properly evaluate your sales efforts and determine what works and what doesn't unless every staff member uses the same presentation and procedures consistently. I recommend that you script the entire presentation. Develop lead lines, benefit statements and product information that clearly explain what is important about your company, products and services. Brainstorm answers to the most common objections and outline some closing statements. Put it in writing and make everyone memorize it. Let each person conform it to their own selling personality, but insist that the basic ideas are used consistently by every member of the sales team.

Special tips for selling at consumer shows

For those of you who exhibit in public and retail consumer shows, here are four sales techniques you can use to increase the dollar amount of every transaction and increase repeat and mail order sales.

Add-ons

Take a tip from your local burger joint. What does the teenager at the cash register ask you after you order your sandwich? "Would you like fries with that?" That is a perfect example of add-on selling. It is so easy to sell more to someone ready to buy. Be prepared to combine, pair, match and accessorize the original purchase before the sale is complete. If they buy a necklace show them the matching bracelet. If they buy the sunglasses show them the waterproof case. When they buy the fishing rod sell them the tackle box. Make it easy for them to buy more. Keep impulse items close to the cash register. Think of all the gum, magazines, Chapstick and batteries you added to your purchase while waiting for your turn in the checkout line at the grocery store. Always ask for that extra sale.

Labels

Print several hundred peel and stick labels with your company name, phone number, email address and website on them. Place a label on the inside, under side or back side of every product you sell. These serve as the perfect reminder of where to get another one of your great products. They also travel to a new prospect when your items are given as gifts.

Hangtags

Consider the personality of your product, then create something that you can tie, pin on or somehow attach to what you sell that will be worth saving by the purchaser. A creative card with care instructions can be pinned to your silk scarves. A recipe or ingredients can accompany your spice shakers. Include a poem or interesting tidbits about your company along with your contact information. If they love your product they will hang on to the hangtag until they are ready to reorder.

Reorder forms

Make it easy and convenient for a customer to buy from you again and conserve brochures at the same time. Create an easy to fill out order form that can be mailed or faxed back to you when more of your product is needed. Put them into every bag or give them out after every sale.

Sales worksheet

Use the worksheet on the following page to brainstorm with your sales crew and develop a presentation that elicits the information you need to win the customer and close the sale.

SALES WORKSHEET

Goals to Accomplish

1. _____

2. _____

3. _____

Lead Lines to Engage the Customer

1. _____

2. _____

3. _____

Benefits to Excite

1. _____

2. _____

3. _____

Features to Educate

1. _____

2. _____

3. _____

Exit Lines

1. _____

2. _____

3. _____

Target your audience

When you consider the fact that you have to filter through hundreds of prospects to find those that are interested in what you offer, then narrow the field even further to those qualified to purchase what you offer, you begin to realize how critical it is to understand your customer profile. Knowing the type of customer most likely to purchase your product will help you select events that will be attended by people in your target audience. Take time to develop a customer profile by listing the characteristics of the type of person that buys your product or uses your service. Also note what industry or companies your buyer is drawn from. Consider some of the following categories to help you zero in on your customer biography. When evaluating the business, think about the type of industry, size of the company, geographic location, budget restrictions and sales volume. When selling to individuals, look at age, sex, hobbies, rank, position of authority, buying power, decision-making ability and income level. After you evaluate and isolate what characterizes a good prospect, then seek the events most likely to attract that type of person or company.

Selling strategies

You may not realize it, but there are good and bad ways to position and utilize your booth staff. Where your staff is stationed should be determined by the goals that are set and how the traffic flows through or past your exhibit. To get the maximum productivity from your crew, consider the following selling strategies and select the one that best fits your game plan.

Independent selling

This selling strategy can be used when one or more sales associates are in the booth. Each individual is stationed at the perimeter of the booth. Each person is responsible for capturing the customers' attention, qualifying them, providing them with the pertinent information and obtaining a sale or lead. Each sales associate handles all the selling duties as opposed to sharing the task and rotating with others.

Team selling

One of the most effective ways to work your booth is by implementing a team selling system. Following is a description of how it should work. The sales associates are positioned around the perimeter of the booth. They are the designated greeters. The greeters talk to the prospects that go by and attempt to qualify them. Greeters send the best prospects over to the next station where the presenters are waiting. The presenters are positioned in another area of the booth or at a demonstration station. The presenters give the prospects the sales presentation and obtain the written leads. A variation on this system might have the greeter initiating contact, encouraging prospects to participate in an interactive game or register for a contest, then obtain the lead and send them over to the presenter who explains the product or provides a demonstration. Staff members can periodically switch positions to stay fresh. This selling technique works well in both large and small booths allowing for maximum coverage of attendees and minimum burnout of the exhibit staff.

Top tradeshow selling tips

- Make eye contact. Be pro-active. Don't wait for the customer to come to you.

- Selling is a numbers game. Talk to as many people as possible.

- Be enthusiastic and smile often.

- Know your product and how it compares to the competition.

- Script a formal sales presentation.

- Prepare lead lines to engage a prospect in conversation.

- Create a benefit list to excite and educate the customer about your offerings.

- Anticipate objections and plan your responses.

- Develop closing statements.

- Require the staff to memorize the presentation and use it consistently.

Proper etiquette keeps you professional

I bet nobody told you there are rules of etiquette that govern the tradeshow floor. Sometimes we have to go back to the basics and take inventory of our presentation and attitude when we exhibit. Adhering to these simple rules will result in a better impression of your exhibit staff by the attendees. Upon reviewing them, they may seem like common sense considerations everyone should be familiar with. Unfortunately, you will find numerous infractions at every event. Think about how many times you have witnessed them, or worse yet, committed these blunders. The overall image of your company and staff will benefit greatly if you avoid these infractions at your next tradeshow or consumer event. Use these suggestions as a guideline for anyone representing your company at the show.

- **Don't sit down.** Always be up and ready to meet the prospect and make eye contact. Take the chairs out of the booth altogether. A chair in your booth will allow the staff to sit encouraging laziness and making them appear unapproachable. Chairs also welcome attendees to sit down for a rest in your space. If you must sit then at least use a stool you can slide unnoticed under a counter. When someone needs to take a break, have that person leave the booth instead of sitting.

- **Don't leave the booth unattended.** When you must work alone, there are times when you absolutely must leave the booth unattended. Avoid leaving for extended periods, but when you must go, place a sign for everyone to see indicating the time you will return. Don't just tell them you will be back in 15 minutes because they won't know when you left and you could miss an interested prospect. Make sure you tell them the exact time you will return so they can stop back by the exhibit to meet with you.

- **Don't talk excessively to colleagues.** A prospect is not likely to interrupt your conversation for information. Limit the chatter with other staff members to times when prospects are not in view. Stay off the cell phone in the booth. If you must accept or make a call, walk away from the booth area.

- **Don't eat or drink at the booth.** Glasses of soda and plates of food on the front counter look tacky and unprofessional. So do you with a mouthful of food. Step away for a few minutes to enjoy your snack and hide drinks from customers. Gum chewing is distracting and unprofessional, so avoid it and use a breath mint instead.

- **Don't overstaff your exhibit.** It is very intimidating to pass a 10' exhibit where four men in suits are standing on the aisle with their arms folded looking ready to pounce on the next person they see. Whether you are in an island exhibit or a small inline booth space, be aware of the impression made by the location of your employees and how they appear to attendees. The general rule is no more than two people per 100 square feet of exhibit space.

- **Don't knock the competition.** Always sell your product or service on its own merits. Today's savvy consumers resent negative attacks on competition and want you to sell them on your benefits. Strive to keep your integrity intact.

- **Don't act or speak negatively.** When a show is going poorly we look for something to blame. Negative comments are unproductive. Instead, evaluate the cause and how it could be improved. Watch your body language. Nothing is more annoying than a neighboring exhibitor who moans, groans, and complains about the show. Exhibitors have blamed everything from the promoter, the advertising, the customers, the location and the weather for poor show results. Some will try to occupy other exhibitor's time complaining. Negativity like this is unproductive and self-defeating. Even when sales are poor, it is useless to dwell on it. Rather than grumble about a slow show, use the time to make notes on possible reasons why attendance was poor or why your promotions didn't work. Rearrange your merchandise or literature, adjust your sales presentation and check your deodorant. No matter how bored you are, keep your complaints to yourself.

- **Don't monopolize your neighbor.** Sharing ideas and meeting new people is part of the fun of exhibiting, but the first priority is to sell your business. Remember to excuse yourself from your booth neighbor when a client approaches so your neighbor can attend to their visitor.

- **Do arrive early.** Arriving at the booth 30 minutes before the show opens allows you to discover problems and gives you enough time to get ready to meet the public. You will also have time to check out the other exhibits before attendees arrive and restock your inventory and supplies.

- **Do dress the part.** Look successful by dressing in crisp, clean clothes. Your appearance should be stylish and professional and your grooming must be impeccable. If you are not dressed to match a booth theme then dress to stand out from the style of the attendees. Wear comfortable shoes. This one suggestion will save you hours of pain.

- **Do inventory.** Save yourself the panic of running out of important items. At the end of every day take note of what products, selling supplies, marketing materials, business cards and give-aways you will need to restock for the next day.

- **Do come prepared.** Make sure you know what your competition will be doing at the show, have superior product knowledge and an update on all pricing for your business.

- **Do keep the display neat** Empty the garbage, straighten the products, run the vacuum and keep purses and briefcases out of site.

- **Do develop a professional hand shake.** Don't be guilty of the limp lift, the wet noodle or the double-handed squeeze. Be ready to extend your hand, grip theirs in a firm, yet friendly manner, pump three times then release.

- **Do identify yourself.** Every show you attend or exhibit in will issue you a badge with your name and company name printed on it. It may also be color coded to identify you as an exhibitor, buyer, attendee, committee member or services staff. The I.D. badges must be worn at all times and serve to restrict access to those who are not registered to attend the show. When you greet people, you shake their right hand, which places their line of vision over your right shoulder. Wearing your I.D. tag on your right side makes it easier for them to read your name and vice-versa.

  If the badge is issued without your name printed on it, you should make sure the staff has personalized name badges so it is easy for attendees to get to know who they are working with. If you are in a public show like a sportsmen's expo and you sell fishing lures, wear a fish shaped nametag. If yours is a business event then consider a clever LED nametag with name and message running across it like a ticker tape. A clever badge keeps you looking professional and can serve as a conversation starter.

- **Do look approachable.** Smile often, make eye contact and greet prospects by name. Always project a positive and friendly manner. Be conscience of your body language. Body language has a profound impact on the attendees walking by your booth. Make sure your demeanor projects an open, attentive attitude that welcomes prospects your way. Avoid sitting, slouching, or leaning on the display. Be sure to show enthusiasm throughout the day and be as approachable and pleasant at 5 p.m. as you were at 9 a.m.

- **Do greet your neighbor.** Sharing ideas and making friends with other exhibitors is part of the fun associated with exhibit marketing. Just remember though, an exhibitors first priority is to work the show. Exhibitors cannot acknowledge and qualify prospects if they are engaged in discussions with another exhibitor. Customers are often reluctant to interrupt with questions when an exhibitor is talking to someone else. Be alert during conversations with vendors and excuse yourself when a prospect approaches.

Create an Effective Follow-up System

This amazing statistic from the Center for Exhibition Industry Research reinforces the necessity for a formal procedure for following up all those valuable leads you've collected at the shows. The studies revealed that 73 percent of companies that exhibit in tradeshows gather qualified leads, yet 85 percent of those leads never receive post show follow-up.

Don't let your company lose out on the chance to turn those leads into sales. Any leads that have not been sent back to the office for immediate follow-up must be contacted no later than one week from the closing of the show. Make this a mandatory requirement for all sales staff and request a monthly written report charting the follow-up progress on the assigned leads. If you are following up your own leads refer to the ranking category and the notes made at the time of the meeting to remind you of what was discussed, what was needed and what personal tidbit was noted to help jog the prospect's memory when you speak with them. If you are not following up on your own leads, make sure whoever is assigned the task understands the notes and references on each lead and the name of the salesperson who met that person at the show so they can refer to them during the call.

Below are a variety of ideas you can add to your follow-up efforts that may help to close the deal or gather other valuable information from the prospect. Decide in advance whether to contact the prospect by email, phone, fax or mail. Here is a money saving tip to keep in mind. You can mail five, 8½" x 11" sheets of paper in one #10 envelope for the cost of one stamp.

Say thank you

I'm especially impressed with companies that send out thank you notes to attendees who have visited their booth, entered their contest or made a purchase at the show. This special gesture promotes goodwill and helps prospects remember you when they are ready to buy. If the prospect did make a purchase you might consider sending a promotional item along with the thank you note.

Make an announcement

Include interesting information about your company that is not part of the sales pitch. Announce who won the drawing, mention an upcoming anniversary or invite them to an open-house. Give them a calendar marked with the dates of all your future shows. Don't hesitate to brag about your good fortune or share useful and interesting information about you and your company.

Give preferred treatment

If you own a department store credit card then you've received inserts in the mail that tell you about the special sale days prepared just for you because you are one of the store's preferred customers. They don't shut down the store for you, but that acknowledgement does make you feel special. Give your prospects or customers the preferred treatment when you are introducing a new service, policy or product line. Let your customers or a select group of prospects be the first to hear the news and have the option to look over the offer or purchase the item before it goes public. Make it clear in your solicitation that they are receiving special treatment and preferred status. This works well to develop brand loyalty.

Take a survey

If you did not conduct a survey at your booth during the show, consider soliciting your survey response in the follow-up package. Send along a short questionnaire that asks for opinions and information you need for future marketing. You can determine how memorable your branding was by asking if they remember your name and what you sell. Can they recall your marketing message or theme? Ask them questions that will uncover their value as a client and if they have a need for your services. Request information about timeline and budget. If you allow the prospect to answer anonymously, your returns will double. Another way to encourage the return of the survey is to offer a gift for responding by a certain time period. Include a self-addressed, stamped envelope and you will be sure to get a large number of responses.

Ask for referrals

Referrals are the backbone of the sales industry. Unfortunately, most sales people don't remember to ask for referrals. When soliciting a sale or sending information to your prospect list, ask the customer to give you the name and contact information of any person or company that might benefit from your product or service. If you include a gift or incentive for the referral you will increase your responses.

Share publicity

Publicity is very powerful and can lend credibilit'
cause. If you or your company has been lucky enough to geᴛ
an article written about you in the local newspaper, make
copies and include them in your mailings. You can put a list of
the tradeshows you will be exhibiting in over the next few
months at the bottom of the page. If your industry is making
headlines include a copy of the article. Use publicity to your
advantage and share the news.

Solicit testimonials

A complimentary testimonial from a satisfied customer is a
valuable marketing tool. Whenever a client expresses
overwhelming satisfaction with your product or service ask
them to put their kind words in writing on their company
letterhead. You can also solicit responses with your follow-up
materials. Send a form that asks what the customer likes best
about your company, products or employees. Ask permission
to quote them. After you accumulate a variety of responses,
produce a flyer with all the comments and quotes listed. Hand
these out at events, repeat the quotes on company literature
and mail them in your follow-up materials.

Include a call to action

In order to solicit a sale and encourage a purchase when you
follow up a lead, send more than the standard brochure and
sales literature. Include a special incentive to purchase that
will encourage a response and increase sales. Offer a two-for-
one special, a gift with purchase, a percentage off the price,
buy one get one free, free shipping with an order or a gift
certificate. To motivate a prospect to act in rapid fashion,
be sure to include a deadline date by which they must
respond. Don't forget to include a show code in the literature

that will make it easier to track which show the response came from.

Calculate your ROI (return on investment)

When evaluating the results of participation in tradeshows or consumer shows, many businesses will complain that exhibiting events are a waste of time and don't produce sales. When I offer to track the results of a company's efforts, they cannot provide me with accurate documentation. In other words, they have no idea how productive the show was because they have no tracking methods in place. If you are going to spend the money to exhibit, you might as well take the time to put a system in place that can prove the value of your time and investment. Following the progress of the leads you have collected is one way to measure the value of your efforts and demonstrate to management the impact trade shows can have on the bottom line. Develop a system that will follow the progress of each lead for at least six months. Require the staff assigned to the follow-up procedure to provide a written record of the progress of each lead. Document each customer contact. Record the date, time and responses of each phone call or email. At the end of six months, categorize the information and review the findings with the staff. With this information, you will be able to determine what type of leads were obtained, what shows produced the best leads, which employees have the best trade show techniques, what promotions worked and what follow-up style turns leads into sales. Measure your cost per lead by taking your individual show budget, including travel and personnel expenses, and divide it by the number of leads you received. (Example: $100,000 budget divided by 1,000 leads equal $100 per lead.) The industry average is $185 per lead.

Consider creating a form to evaluate each event after it takes place. When you have established a system for measuring and tracking results you can compare one year with the next to weed out unproductive shows and determine where the program needs improvement. Keep a record on each show and tabulate the totals in these categories. The number of leads collected, amount of press received, the number of appointments made, traffic to the booth, attendance to a live demo and the effectiveness of the sales presentation. You can even make note of the weather that day and you will begin to see a pattern and have a history that can justify continuing in a show or pulling it from your schedule.

Align your objectives with those desired by attendees. Sophisticated attendees don't waste their time at shows any longer. They research exhibitors on-line before a show and have a game plan before they arrive. If you help attendees find solutions to their problems, help eliminate their pain, provide knowledgeable staff to answer their questions, introduce the latest line of products, offer state of the art technology and provide a way to stay in touch, you will be assured of good results. If you do the necessary research and survey your target audience you should receive the most benefit from your experience and give the most value to your prospects and customers.

THE EXHIBIT EXPERT'S TOP TEN TIPS

1 Plan Ahead
Begin preparations for each event well in advance.
This will save you time, money and headaches.

2 Set Objectives
Know what you want to accomplish at every show. Make
sure the exhibit staff understands what is expected of them.

3 Project a Positive Image
First impressions are critical. Every element of your
display must reflect your company's professionalism and
integrity.

4 Design a Dynamic Display
You have seven seconds to attract attention. For
maximum exposure, coordinate every element of the
display around a theme.

5 Reinforce Your Marketing Message
Use large, colorful graphics with a minimum of text to
illustrate products, services and sales messages.

6 Train Your Staff
80 percent of trade show attendees base their opinion of
your company on the actions of your employees in the
booth.

7 Develop a Sales Strategy
Script a sales presentation that engages, qualifies and
solicits leads. Require staff to memorize and use it.

8 Follow-up Effectively
Contact all leads within one week. Phone, fax, email or
mail information that solicits an appointment or sale.
Include a deadline for reply.

9 Exude Enthusiasm
Nothing makes a better impression than happy, smiling
employees eager to assist inquisitive customers.

10 Factor in Some Fun
Don't be so stuffy. Trade show attendees want to be
entertained, as well as informed. Winners combine the two.

ABOUT THE AUTHOR

When it comes to tradeshows, Susan Ratliff is the Exhibit Expert. Nationally recognized as an authority on tradeshow marketing, Susan learned the exhibit business from the trenches, discovered the shortcuts and made the mistakes so you don't have to. In 1988 she started a home-based personalized children's book business that grew into the 2nd largest distributorship in the country. Susan was learning the exhibit business from the ground floor up, carting her computer and supplies everywhere in search of new clients who would buy her books. One weekend she exhibited in the ballroom of a ritzy hotel surrounded by professionals in business suits. The next weekend she was in the middle of a hot, dusty parking lot selling to tourists in shorts and T-shirts. By participating in many different types of exhibiting events and making every mistake in the book, she learned first-hand what skills were required to be an exhibit expert.

When a divorce forced her to seek additional income she sold the book business and went to work selling portable tradeshow displays for a company representing the popular Featherlite Brand of exhibits. When her boss decided to retire and sell the business, Susan jumped at the chance to buy her own professional display company. As president of Exhibit Experts, Susan knows what works at shows and how to save your company time and money. She has a rare and valuable perspective on the industry from both sides of the fence as an exhibitor selling a product and as a supplier providing the tools to be successful at a show. You will exhibit like a pro using her formulas for success.

Since capitalizing on that lucky opportunity, Exhibit Experts has become one of the most successful and highly recognized display companies in Arizona providing exceptional products and extensive resources that help companies look great, sell better and make more money at tradeshows, consumer shows and events. Susan Ratliff is an award-winning entrepreneur receiving numerous awards including Small Business Owner of the Year and the Pioneer awards from National Association of Women Business Owners (NAWBO) and the Sterling Award from the Scottsdale Chamber of Commerce. Susan is a published author, a charismatic speaker on topics that benefit small business owners and is co-host of a weekly radio program called the Small Business Power Hour on KFNN radio in Phoenix, Arizona. In addition, Susan is the founder of the successful Women Entrepreneurs' Small Business Boot Camp. This full day conference celebrates the accomplishments of local micro business owners and provides education and motivation to help them battle their most difficult business challenges.

Like most entrepreneurs, Susan has weathered many business challenges and survived to tell about them. She enjoys sharing the valuable, hands-on experience she has accumulated from both sides of the exhibit aisle. Her husband, Carey, who has years of experience supervising, installing and dismantling exhibits contributes his valuable perspective about the exhibit industry. To learn more about Susan Ratliff or for resources to help you grow your business, visit the following websites:

www.exhibitexpertsaz.com

www.susanratliff.com

www.womensbusinessbootcamp.com

www.smallbusinesspowerhour.com

How to order additional books:

By phone: 602-437-3634

By fax: 602-437-0955

On line: www.exhibitexpertsaz.com

By mail: Simply photocopy this form and return it to

Susan Ratliff

Exhibit Experts

4012 E. Broadway, Suite 307

Phoenix, Arizona 85040

_____copies of *Exhibit Like An Expert* @ $20 each   _____
                                                 includes tax

S/H $3 per book   _____

Total enclosed   _____

Name _____

Address _____

City_____State_____Zip_____

Email_____

Payment:

Check or money order payable to Susan Ratliff

Type of card ❏ Visa   ❏ Mastercard   ❏ American Express

Card number _____

Name on card _____

Expiration date _____

CNN Security #_____

(3 digits on the back of Visa and MC, 4 digits on the front of AmEx)

Cardholder signature _____

Dedication to be written in books   _____

_____

Looking for a motivational speaker for your next event?

If you would like to hire Susan Ratliff to give one of the following, energetic, informative presentations at your next event, you can reach Susan at 602-437-3634 or e-mail her at Susan@exhibitexpertsaz.com

Tradeshow Tactics to Maximize Your Prospects and Profits

- Design a display that gets you noticed
- Plan promotions that steal the show
- Learn sales strategies that get results
- Receive tips that will save you money

Network Your Way to the Bank

- Discover the art of networking
- Become a referral guru
- Make your message memorable
- Expand your sphere of influence

How To Get Your Name in the News

- Experience the power of publicity
- Get it, manipulate it, maximize and exploit it
- Have the media calling on you
- Create credibility for your cause

How to Succeed When You Don't Feel Successful (keynote)

- Learn ten lessons for conquering challenges
- Turn obstacles into ammunition
- Discover how to beat the odds and achieve your dreams
- Strengthen your power to succeed